U0686167

板蓝根　藿香　鱼腥草

杏仁　甘草　石膏　大黄

红景天　金银花　连翘

麻黄　贯众　薄荷

"書法小聯合國" 书法文化特色课程

Special Course on Calligraphy Culture
by Junior United Nations of Calligraphy

"书法·小篆合图" 书法文化特色课程

Special Course on Calligraphy Culture

by Junior United Nations of Calligraphy

本成果系教育部哲学社会科学研究重大课题攻关项目"中国书法文化国际传播的理论与实践研究"（项目编号：2016JZD031）、2020年上海市文化走出去专项扶持资金"后疫情时代联合国汉字文化推广与系列网络课程开发"和教育部中外语言交流合作中心国际中文教育研究课题一般项目"国际中文教育和中国书法文化传播融合研究"（项目批准号20YH02C）阶段性成果。

風調雨順·國風

编著：周斌　杨柏灿　周佳楠

封面题字：周斌

插图：孙凌雁

书法：盛兰军

书籍设计：周海波

翻译：韩丑萍　胡子曦

华东师范大学出版社

上海

图书在版编目（CIP）数据

风调雨顺.国风 / 周斌，杨柏灿，周佳楠编著 . — 上海：华东师范大学出版社，2021
ISBN 978-7-5760-1726-7

Ⅰ.①风… Ⅱ.①周… ②杨… ③周… Ⅲ.①中华文化—青少年读物②汉字—书法—文化
—中国—青少年读物 Ⅳ.①K203-49 ②J292.1-49

中国版本图书馆 CIP 数据核字 (2021) 第 086175 号

风调雨顺·国风

编　　著　周　斌　杨柏灿　周佳楠
策划编辑　王　焰
组稿编辑　龚海燕
责任编辑　宣晓凤
审读编辑　李贵莲
责任校对　张佳妮
封面设计　冯逸珺

出版发行　华东师范大学出版社
社　　址　上海市中山北路 3663 号　邮编 200062
网　　址　www.ecnupress.com.cn
电　　话　021-60821666　行政传真　021-62572105
客服电话　021-62865537　门市 (邮购) 电话　021-62869887
地　　址　上海市中山北路 3663 号华东师范大学校内先锋路口
网　　店　http://hdsdcbs.tmall.com

印 刷 者　上海盛隆印务有限公司
开　　本　700 × 1000　12 开
印　　张　12
字　　数　56 千字
版　　次　2021 年 7 月第 1 版
印　　次　2021 年 7 月第 1 次
书　　号　ISBN 978-7-5760-1726-7
定　　价　98.00 元
出 版 人　王　焰

（ 如发现本版图书有印订质量问题，请寄回本社客服中心调换或电话 021-62865537 联系 ）

中医药科普专家指导委员会

黄震　胡鸿毅　陈红专　张伟民

目录

各位大小朋友们，你们认识它们吗？

它们是熊猫妮妮和小鸡杰瑞，妮妮与杰瑞是一对好朋友。妮妮生活在中国，杰瑞生活在国外。它们不仅每年写信问候彼此，而且今年妮妮还邀请了杰瑞一起来中国过春节，它们包饺子、贴春联，度过了一个非常愉快的春节。

杰瑞想要了解更多的中国文化，便向知名老中医妮妮的爷爷请教。妮妮的爷爷说，中药是中国传统文化的典型代表，可以从了解中药开始来学习中国文化。于是妮妮带着杰瑞来到了位于上海中医药大学内的中医药博物馆和百草园。讲解员生动的讲解，使杰瑞仿佛在上下五千年的历史长河中来回穿越，它被中医药的博大精深深深地吸引。它决定开启一次在中国的中医药之旅。

Dear friends, do you know Nini the Panda and Jerry the Chicken?

They are two good friends. Nini lives in China and Jerry lives abroad. They write letters to each other regularly. This year Nini invited Jerry to China for the Spring Festival. They made dumplings, pasted up spring couplets and had a wonderful Chinese New Year.

Jerry wanted to learn more about Chinese culture. It asked Nini's grandfather for advice. Nini's grandfather is a well-known doctor of traditional Chinese medicine (TCM). It suggested that a good place to start would be to look into TCM since it's inherently rooted in Chinese culture. Nini and Jerry took its advice and visited the TCM Museum and Herbal Garden at the campus of Shanghai University of Traditional Chinese Medicine. With the vivid explanation of the guide, walking around the TCM museum is a tour of 5000 years of history. Deeply fascinated by its profoundness, Jerry decided to embark on a new journey to discover traditional Chinese medicine in China.

妮妮和杰瑞首先来到了邻近上海的浙江杭州。在前往中国前，杰瑞一直听说中国的丝绸举世闻名，妮妮便邀请杰瑞一起前往坐落于杭州西湖边的中国丝绸博物馆参观。

　　一进博物馆，杰瑞便被丝绸的制作工艺所折服，同时也对这绫罗绸缎中五彩缤纷的颜色感到好奇，饶有兴致地询问妮妮："妮妮，这布料上的颜色是怎么染上去的呀？"

　　"古代主要是用植物染料进行上色的，比如红色用的是红花和茜草，黄色用的是栀子和黄柏。"妮妮回答。

Nini and Jerry first visited the city of Hangzhou in Zhejiang Province neighbouring Shanghai. Before its trip to China, Jerry had heard that Chinese silk is well known to the world. So Nini took Jerry to the China National Silk Museum, which is located near the West Lake in Hangzhou.

Upon entering the museum, Jerry was amazed at the craftsmanship and beautiful colours of the silk."Nini, how did the colours get into the fabric?" asked Jerry with eagerness.

"In ancient times, dyes were originally derived from trees or plants. For example, red came from safflowers and Indian madder roots, and yellow came from Cape jasmine fruit and phellodendron bark." Nini replied.

"哦，好像很多都是中药材呢！那这蓝色用的是什么呢？"杰瑞指着一件蓝色长衫继续追问。

"古代的蓝色染料是青黛，嗯……是植物菘蓝的叶子经浸泡、石灰搅拌、晾晒碾粉等过程加工而成的。"妮妮思考片刻后说道。

"菘蓝？这也是一味中药吗？好像没有听说过。"杰瑞有些疑惑地问道。

妮妮笑着说："是的，菘蓝或许你不熟悉，但是它的根你一定有所耳闻，就是中药板蓝根。"

"Oh, many of them are Chinese materia medica! So what about this blue colour?" Jerry went on, pointing to a blue gown.

"Indigo. Well, it was derived from the leaves of dyer's woad herb, isatis tinctoria and processed by soaking in lime water and grinding into powder." Nini thought for a moment and said.

"Woad? Is it also a Chinese herb? I've never heard of it." Jerry asked doubtfully.

Nini smiled and said, "Yes. You probably haven't heard of woad. But you must have heard of its root — isatis root."

"板蓝根呀！这我听说过，好像对于流感的治疗效果很好呢！"杰瑞恍然大悟地说。

"没错，板蓝根有着很好的清热解毒作用，对于流感的预防和治疗可以说已经是家喻户晓了。另外，板蓝根还有一个特点，它能够清利咽喉，对于流感引起的咽喉肿痛特别有效。"妮妮骄傲地说。

"原来如此，这染料背后也有着这么多中医药的奥秘呀，这次博物馆之旅真的是受益匪浅。"杰瑞心满意足地说。

"Isatis root! I've heard of it. It works well for influenza! " Jerry suddenly realized it does know this root.

"You are right. It acts to clear heat and remove toxins, and is therefore often used for influenza prevention and treatment. Additionally, it also benefits the throat, especially for influenza-related sore throat. " Nini said proudly.

"I see. There is so much TCM knowledge behind these dyes. I learned a great deal from this museum trip. " Jerry said contentedly.

板蓝根。

板蓝根 ○ Isatis root

产地：主产于河北、江苏、安徽等地。
性味：苦、寒。
功效：清热解毒，清利咽喉。
应用：① 防治呼吸道传染病，如流感。
　　　② 风热感冒所出现的咽喉肿痛。

基本信息
Essential information

Places of production: Hebei, Jiangsu, Anhui, etc.

Medicinal properties: Bitter in flavor and cold in nature.

Actions: Clears heat, removes toxins, and benefits the throat.

Indications: ① Prevention & treatment of infectious respiratory diseases
　　　　　　 such as influenza.

　　　　　　 ② Sore, swollen throat in common cold due to wind-heat.

篆书 (zhuan shu) | Seal script

篆书"板"字为形声字。"木"是形符，"反"是声符。"反"意为"镜像对称的事物或动作"。"木"指薄木板。"木"与"反"联合起来表示"建筑物的隔板"。

In the seal script, "板 (ban)" is a pictophonetic character. The left part "木 (mu)" is the semantic element, meaning thin wooden boards. The right part "反 (fan)" is the phonetic element, meaning things or movements that are symmetrical in mirror image. The character "板 (ban)" means separating wooden boards used in buildings.

篆书"蓝"字为形声字。上部分"艹"为形符，"监"为声符。本义是蓼(liǎo)蓝草，蓼蓝草叶子的汁液可以提取蓝色的染料。

In the seal script, "蓝 (lan)" is a pictophonetic character. The top part "艹" is the semantic element. The bottom part "监 (jian)" is the phonetic element. The original meaning of character "蓝 (lan)" is an indigo plant, whose leaves can make blue dyes.

篆书"根"为形声字。"木"是形符，"艮(gèn)"是声符。其含义是植物茎干下部长在土里的部分。

In the seal script, "根 (gen)" is a pictophonetic character. The left part 木 is the semantic element. The right part "艮 (gen)" is the phonetic element. The original meaning of character "根 (gen)" is a part of a plant that grows downward into the soil.

书法基本笔画
示范视频

跟着妮妮写一写
Practice calligraphy with Nini

楷书（kai shu）| Regular script

一 十 才 才 木 术 杤 杤 板

丨 十 十 艹 艹 艹 艹 芦 芦 芦
芦 莳 莳 莳 莳 蔜 蔜 蕳
藍

一 十 才 才 木 术 村 村 根
根 根

靛蓝染布

药青燥主为柏料，大干的"蓝"染料很大，板蓝根大为紫色的染料等。栀子、黄柏为紫色染料，板蓝根入药所得的染料胜于"蓝"中的亦加出蓝而来自板蓝根中的药材，如片处理后加工染出于蓝而胜于"蓝"中所用的染料，紫苏染料叶片代青就来自板蓝根中的染色中所用的染色其工是古"青"就"蓝"—靛蓝。药材，加黛。"青"加工是过青一个"蓝"就来自板蓝根中的饰中药材，紫草为红色部，其工是那个"蓝"—靛蓝。服饰中紫草根经青之其加工是红料过青加一个"蓝"传统服饰染色中所用的药材经青一个"蓝"—靛蓝。传统来源于染料，茜草为红色料，紫草根经茎即部分来源于染料，茜草为茎即叶，那即是原料中的部分黄红花、茜草茎即叶，原料中的部分黄红花用叶粉末要中的"蓝"—靛蓝。

将板蓝根发酵之后把色素提取出来可以进行着色。在古代，布料还需要最后再放入水里面煮，然后晒干，上图案，最后再放入染缸着色，数次后完成染色。

Traditionally, most fabric dyes are derived from Chinese medicinal plants. For example, yellow came from Cape jasmine fruit and phellodendron bark, purple came from arnebia roots and perilla leaves, and red came from safflowers and Indian madder roots. Both the roots (Radix Isatidis) and leaves (Folium Isatidis) of the plant are of medicinal use. The dried powder processed from its stems and leaves is called qīng dài (Indigo Naturalis), one of the main sources for indigo blue dye. There is an old saying in Chinese, "Indigo blue is extracted from the indigo plant, but is bluer than the plant it comes from." The "blue" here comes from the woad plant.

The dyeing process includes woad fermentation, pigment extraction and coloring. In ancient times, people boiled fabrics in water, hung the fabrics up to dry, ironed designed patterns onto the fabrics, and then placed them back to the dye vat. The entire dyeing process has to be performed several times.

Dyeing fabrics with indigo

13

虽然已是春天，但依然有一丝寒意，妮妮和杰瑞决定去春暖花开的广州。

这天，它们来到一个植物生长茂盛的地方。妮妮指着不远处散发着阵阵芳香的绿色植物兴奋地说："杰瑞，你知道那是什么吗？那是一味有名的中药，叫藿香。"

杰瑞好奇地问："它为什么叫藿香？"

妮妮说："藿香主要在春夏季节生长旺盛，能散发出阵阵香气，人们闻了这股香味以后，会感到神清气爽，食欲大开。因为以广东产的藿香质量最好，所以又叫广藿香。"

"哦！"杰瑞若有所思，接着问道，"你刚才说它是一味中药，它有什么作用吗？能治疗什么病？"

Although it is spring, it's still a little bit chilly. Nini and Jerry decided to go to Guangzhou, (often known as Canton, the capital city of southern China's Guangdong Province) to experience the warm spring with blooming flowers.

One day they came to a place full of thriving plants. Nini pointed at some aromatic green plants and asked excitedly, "Jerry, do you know what that plant is? It is a well-known Chinese herb called patchouli."

Jerry asked curiously, "Why is it called patchouli?"

妮妮说道："这说起来可就话长了。在中国每年到了农历四五月份，一些地区的气温越来越高，雨水也越来越多，整个环境闷热潮湿。一些冬眠于地下的蜈蚣、蝎子等生物逐渐苏醒，随地出没，它们的分泌物、排泄物含有毒素，作用于人体后能引发一些疾病，有些还具有传染性；特别是随着天气越来越热，蚊虫、苍蝇的滋生、繁殖也越来越快，会引起一些疾病的发生和传播，中医称之为瘟疫。"

Nini said, "Patchouli thrives in summer and spring. It is best known for its strong and thick aroma. Its aroma helps to increase our appetite and makes us feel refreshed. Guangdong has the best Patchouli across China."

"Oh!" Jerry nodded and continued to ask, "Did you just say it is a Chinese herb? What are its actions and indications?"

Nini replied, "That's a long story. During every fourth and fifth lunar months, many places across China are warm, rainy, and humid. In such an environment, hibernating creatures including centipedes or scorpions gradually wake up. Their excreta or secretions can contain microorganisms that increase the risk for infectious diseases. In addition, the climatic condition accelerates the breeding of flies and mosquitoes, which also promotes the spread of diseases. This is known as pestilence in Chinese medicine."

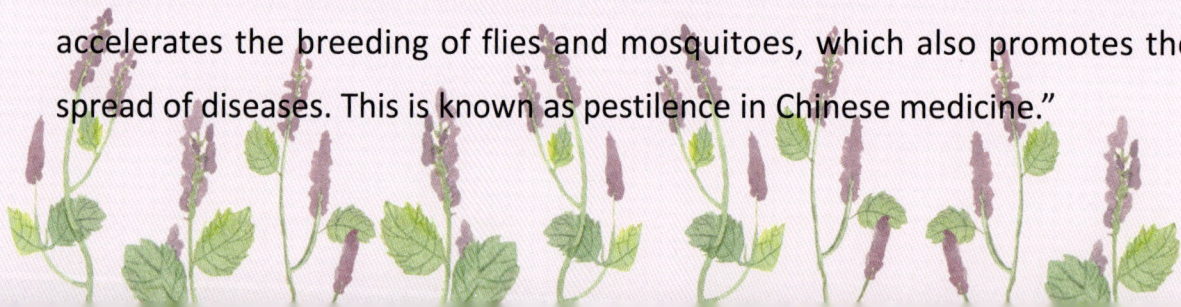

杰瑞皱着眉头说:"哦哦,那有什么解决办法吗?"

"有啊,"妮妮用有点骄傲的口气说,"我们的古人很智慧,中药能有效地解决这些问题。中医认为,自然界中一些气味芳香的中药能很好地预防和治疗这些瘟疫,藿香就是其中的代表。"

妮妮又补充道:"每年的初夏时节,有一部分人会出现不想吃饭、饮食无味、腹胀乏力、四肢困倦等现象,这在中医中称为疰(zhù)夏,藿香对此有非常好的作用。"

"原来是这样啊。中医和中药真是神奇,我以后也要学中医,用中药。"杰瑞认真地说。

Jerry frowned and asked, "Is there a way to deal with it?"

"Yes," Nini said with pride, "Our ancestors were very intelligent. They used aromatic Chinese herbs to prevent and treat these problems, including patchouli."

"At the beginning of each summer, some people may have trouble acclimatizing to the seasonal change and thus experience a poor appetite, abdominal distension and fatigue. Patchouli is very helpful in this regard." Nini added.

"Oh, I see. Chinese medicine is indeed amazing. I will learn about Chinese medicine and someday be able to use Chinese herbs." Jerry said seriously.

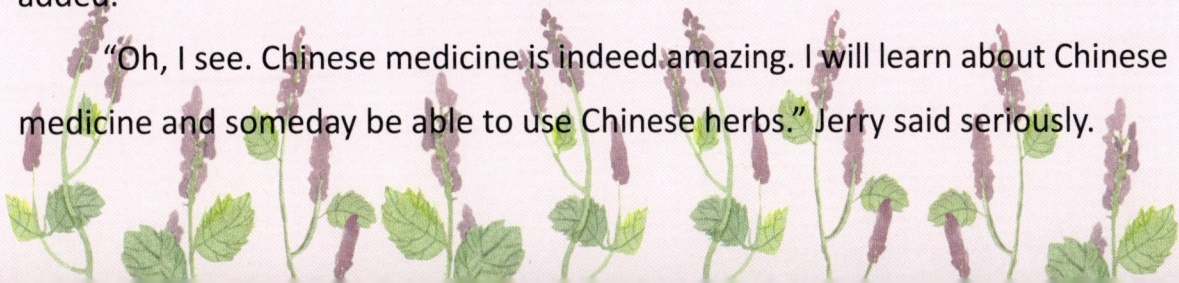

藿香。

藿香 Patchouli

产地：主产于广东、海南等地。

性味：芳香，辛，微温。

功效：芳香健脾、发表散寒、解暑化湿。

应用：① 湿浊困脾引起的食欲不振、口黏乏味、四肢困倦、呕吐泄泻，舌苔白腻。

② 夏季感冒出现的恶寒、头身痛、汗出不畅、肢体困重。

③ 夏季中暑防治。

基本信息
Essential information

Places of production: Guangdong, Hainan, etc.

Medicinal properties: Fragrant and pungent, mildly warm in nature.

Actions: Fortifies the spleen with aroma, releases the exterior, dissipates cold, relieves summer heat and transforms dampness.

Indications: ① A poor appetite, sticky, tasteless feeling in the mouth, fatigue, vomiting, diarrhea and a white, greasy tongue coating due to turbid dampness affecting the spleen.

② Chills, body ache, headache, inhibited sweating and limb heaviness due to common cold in summer.

③ Prevention & treatment of heat stroke in summer.

篆书（zhuan shu）| Seal script

"藿"字为形声字，字从"艹"，从"霍"。"霍"原是会意字，初见于商代甲骨文，上部是雨，下部是一只或几只鸟，群鸟冒雨飞翔会发出霍霍的声响，引申指疾速声，亦指疾速。加上"艹"就成为植物的叶子，特指豆类植物的叶子。

"藿（huo）" is a pictophonetic compound (also called a Semantic-phonetic compound) with "艹" as its semantic radical and "藿（huo）" as its phonetic radical. "藿（huo）" is originally an associative compound which was first discovered on the oracle bone script of Shang dynasty. Its top part "雨（yu）" means rain and its bottom part means birds. Therefore, the whole character originally meant. the sound made by a flock of birds flying in the rain. Later it developed a meaning which is the sound of travelling at a great speed and then it further evolved into meaning to travel at a great speed. When the semantic radical "艹" was added to it, "藿（huo）" came into being, meaning the leaves of a plant, legume to be specific.

"香"字从"禾"和"甘"，合成会意字，表示黍米饭香甜可口的意思。本义是"食物味道好"，引申为"气味好闻"。

"香（xiang）", an associative character consisting of "禾（he）" and "日（ri）", means millets' being sweet and delicious. The original meaning is tastiness of food. The extended meaning is a pleasant smell.

跟着妮妮写一写
Practice calligraphy with Jerry
楷书（kai shu）| Regular script

藿

一 艹 艹 艹 艹 芦 苇 苇 苇
萑 萑 萉 萉 蔖 蔖 蔖 蔖 蔖
藿

香

丿 二 千 禾 禾 禾 香 香 香

香囊

在端午节前后，为了消除梅雨时节的湿浊之邪，佩戴香囊成为其中必不可少的文化元素。香囊，顾名思义，其中多会搭配一些芳香类的药物，通过一些芳香之气来预防蚊虫叮咬及药物传染病的发生。下面将给大家推荐一个端午时节的香囊配方。

取藿香、佩兰、白芷、艾叶、苍术、陈皮各20克，冰片少许，碾成粉末，分装入香囊中，并以棉花填塞，日常可佩于胸前或置于床头，大家一起做做看吧！

It's a cultural tradition to wear Chinese herbal sachets around the Dragon Boat Festival (also known as Duanwu Festival), which was celebrated on the fifth day of the fifth lunar month. The Chinese herbal sachets are filled with pungent or aromatic herbs to prevent infectious diseases and keep good health. Here is a recommended formula for Chinese herbal sachets:

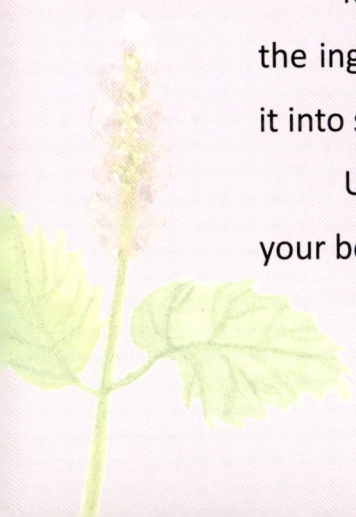

Ingredients: Huo Xiang (Herba Agastachis), Pei Lan (Herba Eupatorii), Bai Zhi (Radix Angelicae Dahuricae), Ai Ye (Folium Artemisiae Argyi), Cang Zhu (Rhizoma Atractylodis), and Chen Pi (Pericarpium Citri Reticulatae), 20 g each.

Making method: Add a small amount of borneol to the ingredients above and grind them into powder, put it into sachets and fill up with cotton.

Usage: Wear the sachet on the chest or put it in your bedroom.

Chinese herbal sachets

告别了广州，杰瑞和妮妮来到了风景秀丽的贵州。它们感叹贵州秀美的风景，也为贵州的风情习俗所感染，最令它们难以忘怀的是一道菜——凉拌鱼腥草。杰瑞对这道菜充满了好奇，边吃边问："妮妮，这个菜为什么叫鱼腥草？"

　　妮妮说："鱼腥草是一味中药，因其新鲜时能散发出如同鱼腥味那样的气味而命名。"

　　"哦。可是它既然是一味中药，怎么又可以做菜呢？"杰瑞不解地问道。

After Guangzhou, Jerry and Nini came to the beautiful city of Guizhou. Besides the beautiful scenery of the region, they were also amazed by the local customs and culture. They were particularly impressed by a local dish—cold houttuynia salad dressed in sauce. Jerry was curious about this dish and asked, "Nini, why is it called houttuynia (*Yuxingcao* in Chinese, which literally means fishy-smelly grass)?"

"It is a Chinese herb. The fresh plant smells fishy." Nini said.

"Oh. But why do you cook it since it is a medicinal plant? " Jerry asked, looking puzzled.

妮妮解释道:"在中药中有一类药物很特别,既可以作为食品食用又可以作为药品应用,称为药食两用品。鱼腥草就是其中之一。

杰瑞若有所思地又问:"鱼腥草有什么作用?"

"Some medicinal plants can be used as both food and medicine. Houttuynia is one of them. " Nini explained.

Jerry asked again thoughtfully, "What's its action?"

妮妮说："鱼腥草的食用主要在西南地区，而且以凉拌为主。"歇了歇，妮妮继续解释道，"西南地区多为山峦盆地，多雨潮湿，到了夏季炎热湿重，多伴热毒、湿毒，对人的健康构成了威胁，特别是多发一些呼吸道的传染性疾病。鱼腥草性寒，具有清热解毒的作用，善于清解呼吸道的热毒，常应用于呼吸道的传染性疾病。"

"哦，原来鱼腥草有这么多功效啊，太好了，我要好好学做这道菜。以后请你吃我做的凉拌鱼腥草！"杰瑞充满向往地承诺。

Nini said, "Houttuynia is mainly eaten as green vegetable (e.g., salad) in southwestern China. In summer times, the regions of mountains and basins in southwestern China are often hot, rainy and humid. Such environment may pose a risk of infectious respiratory diseases. In TCM, houttuyniae is considered cold in nature and thus can clear heat and remove toxins, especially toxic heat in the respiratory tract. Because of this property, it is often used for the treatment of infectious respiratory diseases."

"Wow. What an awesome herb! I'm going to learn to prepare this dish myself and invite you to taste it one day." Jerry promised, its eyes glittering like two stars.

鱼腥草。

鱼腥草 ○ Houttuynia

产　地：主产于浙江、江苏、四川、贵州等地。
性　味：辛，微寒。
功　效：清热解毒，清肺止咳，利尿通淋。
应　用：① 防治呼吸道疾病，如流感、禽流感。
　　　　② 治疗热性咳嗽，如急性气管炎、咽
　　　　　喉炎、肺炎。
　　　　③ 治疗出现尿频、尿急、尿痛的淋证，
　　　　　如泌尿系感染。

Places of production: Zhejiang, Jiangsu, Sichuan, Guizhou, etc.

Medicinal properties: Pungent in flavor and mildly cold in nature.

Actions: Clears heat, removes toxins, clears the lung, stops coughing, promotes urination, and alleviates stranguria.

Indications: ① Prevention & treatment of infectious respiratory diseases such as influenza and bird flu.

② Heat-related cough such as acute bronchitis, pharyngitis or pneumonia.

③ Stranguria (frequent, urgent and painful urination) in urinary tract infection.

篆书 (zhuan shu) | Seal script

篆书"鱼"字从外形看像一条鱼，字的上端是鱼头，中间是鱼身，两旁有鳍，下端是分叉的。

In the seal script, the character "鱼 (yu)" looks like a fish: the top part is its head, the middle part is its body trunk with fins, and the bottom part is bifurcated.

形声字，"月"是形符，"星"是声符。本义指鱼的腥味。引申指"各种肉的异味"。

"腥 (xing)" is a pictophonetic character: "月 (yue)" is the semantic element and " 星 (xing)" is the phonetic element. Its original meaning is the fishy smell. The extended meaning is a bad smell of rotten meat.

形声字，"草"字的上部表示这是草本植物，是形符。字中的"早"部件是声符。其本义是栎实，即栎树的果实，又指春天最先萌芽生长的植物，也可以指草本植物。

"草 (cao)" is a pictophonetic character: the top part is the semantic element, meaning grass or plant; the bottom part "早 (zao)" is the phonetic element. The original meaning is acorn (fruit of the oak tree). It is also the earliest plant to sprout in spring. In addition, it also refers to herbaceous plants.

跟着妮妮写一写
Practice calligraphy with Nini
楷书（kai shu）│ Regular script

鱼 丿 ⺈ ⺈ 鱼 鱼 鱼 鱼 鱼 鱼 鱼 鱼

腥 丿 月 月 月 胛 胛 胛 胛 腥 腥 腥 腥

草 丶 十 艹 艹 艹 芇 苩 苩 草 草

31

凉拌折
耳根

如果大家能够忍受鱼腥草的鱼腥之味的话，不妨也可以用鱼腥草的根来动手做一道西南地区的道地美食——凉拌折耳根！

主料：新鲜折耳根 250 克。

配料：鲜酱油、辣椒油、香油、花椒油、白砂糖、醋、蒜泥适量。

步骤：将新鲜折耳根洗净沥干，切段置于盘内，将上述配料根据自己的口味拌匀即可。

If you are okay with the fishy smell of houttuynia, let's prepare a well-known dish in southwestern China—cold houttuynia salad.

Major ingredient: fresh houttuynia 250 g.

Toppings: fresh soy sauce, pepper oil, sesame oil, Chinese prickly ash oil, white sugar, vinegar, and minced garlic.

Making method: Clean the fresh houttuynia under running water, dry it, and then cut it into pieces. Place the pieces into a plate and mix with the above toppings.

Cold houttuynia salad

趁着春暖花开之际，妮妮与杰瑞来到了"杏乡"新疆伊犁，此时正是杏花绽放的时候，当地举办了盛大的杏花节。坐在开满杏花的树下，妮妮问杰瑞："杰瑞，你知道中国历史上与'杏'有关的典故有哪些吗？"

杰瑞摇了摇头。

妮妮继续说道："在中国历史上与教学有关的叫'杏坛'，而与医学有关的叫'杏林'，主要是为了纪念两位名人：孔子与董奉。"

"孔子我知道，可董奉我不太清楚。"杰瑞说。

During the warm spring, Nini and Jerry came to the town known as Ili in Xinjiang Uygur Autonomous Region. Ili is particularly known for its apricots. When Nini and Jerry visited, there was a grand apricot flower festival taking place. Sitting under a flowering apricot tree, Nini asked Jerry, "Jerry, do you know any Chinese expressions related to the apricot?"

Jerry shook its head.

Nini continued, "There are two apricot-related terms in Chinese history. The one associated with education is called Apricot Altar, and the one associated with medicine Apricot Forest. The former is to commemorate Confucius (551—479 BC), while the latter is to commemorate Dong Feng (220—280)."

"I've heard of Confucius, but I've never heard of Dong Feng." Jerry said.

"董奉是东汉时期的一个大医学家，与张仲景、华佗并称为建安三神医。他不但医术高超而且医德高尚，找他看病的人不计其数，但他不问贵贱、分文不收，只要求他所治愈的病人在他诊所四周种植杏树。病情轻的种一棵，重的种五棵。很快，在他诊所四周的杏树蔚然成林。当杏树成熟结果时，董奉在杏林边搭建了一座谷仓，用杏果交换粮食，董奉再用粮食救济一些穷人。由此诞生了一个著名的成语'杏林春暖'以赞誉董奉，此词一直沿用至今，成为医学界技艺高超、医德高尚的代名词。"妮妮有声有色地讲道。

"Dong Feng was a highly skilled doctor in the period of the Three Kingdoms. He and other two well-known doctors, Zhang Zhongjing and Hua Tuo, were called the 'Three Miracle Doctors' of that period. During the day, he treated patients but charged no fees. Instead, he asked them to plant apricot trees—five if they had been cured from a serious illness and one if they had been cured from a general malady. Many patients came to see him daily, keeping him very busy. After several years, the planted trees created a forest that housed many birds and beasts. When apricots matured, he stored those in a warehouse. Exchanging the apricots for rice, he could then help people with financial difficulties. Dong Feng's apricot forest thus saved numerous lives. Because of his deeds, 'Apricot Forest' becomes another term for the medical community." Nini explained vividly.

"那杏有没有药用价值呢？"杰瑞紧接着问。

"杏果的仁就是杏仁，是一味非常常用的治疗咳喘和便秘的药物。"

"我记住'杏林春暖'这个成语了，如果我以后做医生，也一定像董奉那样。"杰瑞暗下决心。

"Does apricot have any medicinal value?" Jerry followed up.

"Almond is commonly used for cough, panting and constipation."

"Now I truly understand what 'apricot forest' means. If I ever become a doctor, I will be like Dong Feng." Jerry made up his mind.

杏仁。

38

杏仁 Apricot Kernel

产地：主产于东北、西北、华北。
性味：苦，微温，有小毒。
功效：止咳平喘，润肠通便。
应用：① 一切的咳喘病证，如感冒后咳喘、
　　　急慢性气管炎等。
　　② 肠燥便秘，如老年人习惯性便秘、
　　　产后及术后血虚便秘。

基本信息
Essential information

Places of production: Northeast, northwest and northern areas of China.

Medicinal properties: Bitter in flavor, mildly warm in nature, and mildly toxic.

Actions: Stops coughing, alleviates panting, moistens the intestines and promotes bowel movements.

Indications: ① Cough or panting in common cold or acute/chronic bronchitis.

② Constipation in the elderly or after childbirth/surgery due to blood deficiency.

篆书（zhuan shu）| Seal script

篆书"杏"字由"木"和"口"两个部件组成。"木"字表示其属于树木，"口"字表示其可食用。本义为一种落叶乔木，果实称"杏儿"、"杏子"，酸甜，可食。

In the seal script, the character "杏 (xing)" has two parts: the top part "木 (mu)" means trees or wood, while the bottom part "口 (kou)" means edible. The original meaning of the character is a deciduous tree. Its fruit is edible (sour and sweet), called apricot kernel or seed.

篆书"仁"字由"人"和"二"两个部件组成，"人"为其声符。"仁"字的本义是人与人互相亲爱。

In the seal script, the character "仁 (ren)" has two parts: "人 (ren)" and "二 (er)". The left part "人 (ren)" is the phonetic element. The original meaning of the character is to love one another.

一 十 才 木 木 杏 杏

丿 イ 仁 仁

41

杏仁有甜杏仁、苦杏仁之分。两者都具有止咳平喘的功效，甜杏仁味甘，为药食两用品，止咳作用较缓，以润肺止咳为主，适用于老人体虚及虚劳咳喘者。苦杏仁多作药用，止咳作用较强，但有一定的毒性，用量不宜多。

美味杏仁

杏仁食用的方法很多，可以用来做粥、饼、面包等多种类型的食品，还能搭配其他佐料制成美味菜肴。

Apricot kernels come in two varieties: sweet and bitter. Both can alleviate coughing and relieve panting. The sweet one is used for both food and medicine, while the bitter one is mainly used as medicine. The sweet one acts to moisten the lung and has a mild effect on cough relief. The bitter one has a strong effect on cough relief; however, it can only be taken in a small dose since it contains a toxic compound.

Culinary uses: Apricot kernels can be used to make porridge, pancake, bread, etc.

Delicious
apricot kernel

转眼已到了夏天，妮妮与杰瑞来到了地处西北的宁夏。

刚出机场，在前往宾馆的路上，杰瑞看见路边上写着几句广告词："欢迎来到滩羊之乡盐池""欢迎来到甘草之乡盐池""吃着甘草的滩羊"。它不解地问妮妮："盐池是哪里？滩羊、甘草是什么？"

妮妮说："盐池是宁夏的一个地区，滩羊是宁夏一宝，肉质鲜美，没有膻味，对人体有很好的补益作用。甘草则是生长在西北的中药材，宁夏盐池是主产区。"

"那为什么特别强调吃着甘草的滩羊呢？"杰瑞继续问。

It is already summer when Nini and Jerry came to Ningxia Hui Autonomous Region in northwestern China.

On the way to the hotel, Jerry saw some roadside billboard advertisements saying, "Welcome to Yanchi—the Town of Tan Sheep", "Welcome to Yanchi—the Town of Licorice" and "Tan Sheep Are Eating Licorice". It asked Nini, "Where is Yanchi? What are Tan Sheep and Licorice?"

Nini replied, "Yanchi is a town in Ningxia. Tan sheep is one of the treasures of Ningxia since the sheep's meat is fresh, tasty and not smelly. Licorice is a Chinese herb that grows in northwestern China, especially in the town of Yanchi."

"But why must the Tan sheep eat licorice?" Jerry continued to ask.

"这与甘草的特性有关。生长在西北地区的农作物、中药材多有一个共性，甜度高。这是因为宁夏干旱少雨、日夜温差大而光照充足，种植在这种环境下的作物多根系发达，可汲取富含矿物质的地下水。因此，这些作物不但甜度高而且对人体具有一定的补性，如枸杞子、甘草等。其中以甘草为代表。"妮妮喝了口水继续说，"甘草顾名思义就是甜草，其最大的特性是至甘纯甘。几乎所有的人都喜欢甘味，一是口感怡人，二是甘味具有多种作用，特别是对人体具有补虚作用。甘草对人体具有显著的补气功用，并能止咳、止痛、解毒，是一味应用十分广泛的中药材。"

"It's associated with the properties of the licorice plant. Because of a low rainfall, extreme temperature differences and abundant sunlight, all crops and medicinal herbs in northwestern China share a common feature—high sweetness. Plants grown in such environment need a well-developed root system to absorb water and minerals. As a result, these plants, like wolfberries and licorice, are not only sweet but also can tonify the body. In Chinese, licorice is known as *Gan Cao*, which literally means sweet grass. Everybody loves sweet taste, because it is pleasant and can reinforce the body. As an extensively used Chinese herb, licorice can tonify qi, alleviate coughing, relieve pain and remove toxins."

"哦．我明白了。盐池的滩羊之所以没有膻味，肉质鲜美，能补益人体，就是因为食用了至甘纯甘的甘草。"杰瑞若有所思地点点头。

　　"Oh, I see. Licorice is the reason why the meat of Yanchi Tan sheep is fresh, tasty and not smelly." Jerry nodded.

甘草。

甘草 Licorice

产地：主产于内蒙古、宁夏、甘肃等地。

性味：甘，平。

功效：补气，止咳，缓急，解毒，调和。

应用：① 气虚体质和病证出现神疲乏力、食欲不振、面色苍白、肢体倦怠等。

② 咳嗽多痰，如感冒咳嗽、急慢性气管炎等以及咽喉肿痛。

③ 药物、食物中毒的预防和解毒。

④ 腹部、四肢的痉挛性疼痛。

⑤ 心动悸、脉结代，如心律失常。

基本信息
Essential information

Places of production: Inner Mongolia, Ningxia, Gansu, etc.

Medicinal properties: Sweet in flavor and neutral in nature.

Actions: Tonifies qi, stops coughing, alleviates spasm, removes toxins and moderates other ingredients.

Indications: ① Fatigue, a poor appetite, a pale complexion and limb heaviness due to qi deficiency.

② Cough with profuse phlegm in common cold, acute/chronic bronchitis or sore throat.

③ Prevention & detoxification of drug/food poisoning.

④ Spasmodic abdominal or limb pain.

⑤ Palpitations with a knotted or irregularly intermittent pulse in cardiac arrhythmias.

篆书（zhuan shu）| Seal script

"甘"字本义为"甜"。字的外框原是"口"，中间的短横是指示符号，表示嘴里对食物有甘甜的感觉。

The original meaning of this character is sweet. The primary outline roughly forms the shape of "口 (kou)". The transverse line in the middle is a self-explanatory note, meaning a sweet taste in the mouth.

形声字，"草"字的上部表示这是草本植物，是形符。字中的"早"部件是声符。其本义是栎实，即栎树的果实，又指春天最先萌芽生长的植物，也可以指草本植物。

"草 (cɑo)" is a pictophonetic character in the seal script: the top part is the semantic element, meaning grass or plant; the middle part "早 (zɑo)" is the phonetic element. The original meaning is acorn (fruit of the oak tree). It is also the earliest plant to sprout in spring. In addition, it also refers to herbaceous plants.

一 十 廿 甘 甘

丨 十 艹 艹 艹 苫 苗 草
草

51

甘草
桔梗茶

道地药材是中药领域十分具有特色的文化元素。我国西北地区，干旱少雨，昼夜温差大且光照充足，这样的气候环境使得西北地区作物具有甜味甘能补的特点。除甘草以外，如补气的黄芪、补血的当归、补阴的枸杞、补阳的肉苁蓉等也都属于西北地区的道地药材，无不体现了地域环境对药物的影响。

对于盛产甘草的地方，甘草桔梗茶也是一味操作简单方便的茶饮。将桔梗与甘草按等比例分量共同研磨成末，细筛分包可备泡茶用。

In TCM, authenticated (*Daodi*) herbs are produced in certain areas with better quality and efficacy. Thanks to the low rainfall, extreme temperature differences and abundant sunlight, Chinese herbs that grow in northwestern China have higher sweetness and reinforcing or tonifying property. Besides Gan Cao (licorice root), examples include Huang Qi (radix astragali) to reinforce qi, Dang Gui (radix angelicae sinensis) to tonify blood, Gou Qi (fructus lycii) to nourish yin and Rou Cong Rong (herba cistanches) to warm yang.

Licorice and platycodon root tea is easy to make: to grind the platycodon root and licorice (1:1) into powder, sift the powder and place it into tea bags.

Licorice and platycodon root tea

经过连续几个月的旅游，妮妮和杰瑞都感到比较疲劳，决定前往有着"天府之国"之称的四川成都休整一下。

一到成都，它们就被成都的文化深深吸引，成都的美食更是让它们"爱不释口"，尤其是一道"麻婆豆腐"，成为它们每餐必食之菜。杰瑞对豆腐产生了极大的兴趣，缠着妮妮给它解释。

妮妮如数家珍般地说了起来："大概在公元 200 年到 400 年左右，炼丹养生十分盛行，

After months of non-stop traveling, Nini and Jerry became tired. They decided to go to Chengdu, the "Land of Abundance" (because of the fact that it is one of primary food production bases in China) for a few days of rest and relaxation.

As soon as they arrived in Chengdu, they were immediately fascinated by the local culture. What's more, they really loved the local food, particularly a must-eat dish called "mapo tofu" (soft and tender tofu pieces mixed in with ground pork while being seasoned with a bunch of spice). Jerry became extremely interested in Tofu and wanted to know more.

This was something that Nini knew about, "Between 200 ACE and 400 ACE, people were crazy about alchemical elixirs promoting longevity,

前朝君王刘邦的孙子刘安也是其中一员。当时人们认为自然界的矿石吸纳了天地精华，服石养生能使人长生不老，因而许多矿石都被用来炼制长生不老的仙丹，其中就包括了石膏。

"在一次炼丹过程中，刘安无意间将热豆浆翻入了石膏之中。待他再去看时，惊讶地发现豆浆竟结成了块状！

"刘安认为这或许就是仙丹了，于是便尝了一口，感觉异常美味，这就是现在所吃的豆腐的前身。可以说刘安炼丹求仙不成，却无心插柳促成了豆腐的诞生，而他也被誉为'豆腐的始祖'。"

including Liu An, the grandson of the founder of the Han Dynasty. They believed that a man may prolong his life or become immortal by taking medicines made from natural ores or minerals, because these ores or minerals absorbed the essence of heaven and earth. As a result, many ores or minerals such as gypsum were used to make longevity elixirs.

"During an alchemical process, Liu An accidentally poured some hot soybean milk into gypsum. To his surprise, the soybean milk soon curded.

"Liu An believed this to be an elixir of life. After tasting the product, he found it extraordinarily delicious. This is the story of how tofu came into being. Liu An later became known as the 'inventor of tofu'."

"啊！真是太奇妙了，我回去也要试着做做看，"杰瑞感叹道，"咦，为什么石膏加到热豆浆中就会结块呢？"

"石膏其实是一味矿石类的中药，性质寒凉，有生用和煅用之分。其中生石膏有显著的清热作用，而煅石膏的主要作用就是收敛。用于豆腐制作的就是煅石膏，寒性的煅石膏放到热豆浆中，能迅速使热豆浆凝固，从而形成豆腐。"妮妮解释道。

"哦，原来石膏不但可以制作豆腐，还能用于疾病治疗。"杰瑞恍然大悟。

"Ah! That's amazing. I will try to make tofu when I get back home," exclaimed Jerry, "But, why does hot soybean milk turn into curds when mixed with gypsum?"

"Actually gypsum is a medicinal mineral with cold/cool properties. Fresh gypsum can significantly clear heat, while dried gypsum mainly astringes or coagulates things. These properties cause the milk to curd and turn into tofu." Nini explained.

"Oh, now I see. Gypsum can be used for the making of tofu, but it also has a role in the treatment of disease." Jerry suddenly understood.

石膏。

石膏 ○ Gypsum

产地：主产于湖北、河南、西藏、四川、甘肃等地。

性味：辛、甘，大寒。

功效：生石膏清热泻火，除烦止渴；煅石膏收敛生肌。

应用：① 高热不退、烦渴不已的病证，如流感、流脑、肺炎等。

② 肺热咳喘。

③ 胃火牙痛、口臭。

④ 皮肤疮疡 (chuāng yáng) 溃烂不收口、湿疹、水火烫伤。

Places of production: Hubei, Henan, Tibet, Sichuan, Gansu, etc.

Medicinal properties: Pungent and sweet in flavor and extremely cold in nature.

Actions: Clears heat, reduces fire, relieves vexation and alleviates thirst. In addition, dried gypsum helps heal wounds and regenerate tissues.

Indications: ① Persistent high-grade fever and thirst in influenza, epidemic encephalitis, pneumonia, etc.

② Cough and panting due to lung heat.

③ Toothache and a foul breath due to stomach fire.

④ Skin sores that have difficulty healing, eczema, burns or scalds.

篆书 (zhuan shu) | Seal script

篆书"石"字上面部件表示山崖，下面的"口"部件表示石块。整个字表示山崖下有石块。

In the seal script, the top part of the character "石 (shi)" means a cliff and the bottom part "口 (kou)" means rocks. This character means rocks under a cliff.

甲骨文"膏"字由"高"和"夕"两部分组成。"高"从外形看像一座高高的楼阁。"夕"，即肉.表示动物油脂。"膏"指脂肪或很稠的糊状的东西。

In the oracle-bone inscriptions, the character "膏 (gao)" consists of two parts: "高 (gao)" and "夕 (xi)". The upper part looks like a tall pavilion. The lower part means animal fat. This character means fat or thick, pasty things.

一 厂 厂 石 石

丶 亠 亠 古 古 古 古 亭
高 高 亭 膏 膏 膏

61

豆腐

　　故事中提到了用石膏制作豆腐的历史典故，接下来就让我们一起学着动手做做看吧！

　　原料：黄豆、水、食用石膏粉。

　　黄豆用清水泡3小时。每100克黄豆加入900毫升水，打成豆浆。将打好的豆浆用纱布过滤豆渣。豆浆烧开，沸腾3次后关火，同时将2.5克石膏粉加入100毫升水后搅拌。待豆浆冷却至95℃，边搅拌边加入石膏水，静置15分钟，豆腐便完成了！

Let's try to prepare tofu!

Ingredients: Soybean, water and edible gypsum powder (as a coagulant).

Making method: 1) Soak the soybean in water for 3 hours; 2) add 900 ml water to every 100g soybean to make the soy milk; 3) discard the solids using cheesecloth; 4) turn off the heat after bringing the soy milk to boil three times (get rid of the foam each time); 5) add 2.5g gypsum powder to 100ml water and stir completely; 6) stir and add gypsum water when the soymilk becomes 95°C; and 7) let it sit for 15 minutes and the tofu is done.

Tofu

在成都休整的日子里，妮妮和杰瑞为当地的美食所倾倒，但也出现了意想不到的情况。接连几天的辛辣饮食，使得杰瑞排便困难，甚是痛苦。

妮妮安慰杰瑞："别急，我去药店给你配一味中药，泡水喝，很快就可以通便。"于是，妮妮去了药店。

During their stay in Chengdu, Nini and Jerry immersed themselves in local food customs; however, after days of eating hot spicy foods, Jerry started to have difficulty passing stools.

With a well-thought-out plan, Nini said, "Don't worry, I will go to the pharmacy to buy you a Chinese herb, and you will be fine shortly after drinking it with warm water."

不一会儿，妮妮配了一味中药回来，用开水冲泡。约10分钟后，妮妮让杰瑞服下。大约过了半小时，杰瑞的肚子一阵疼痛，肠鸣不断，赶紧去上卫生间，很快就解下了大便，多日的痛苦终于消除。欣喜之余，杰瑞好奇地问妮妮："这味药是什么呀？"

妮妮说："这味药就是四川道地的药材大黄，它还有一个特别的名称叫'将军'！"

"为啥叫将军呀？"杰瑞追问。

After a while, Nini came back with the herb and soaked it in boiling water. About ten minutes later, Nini asked Jerry to drink it. After approximately half an hour, Jerry had abdominal pain with bowel sounds, so it rushed to the bathroom and had a complete evacuation of stool. It asked Nini curiously, "What is it?"

Nini said, "It is an authentic herb produced in Sichuan called rhubarb. It also has the special name of 'general'!"

"Why is it called a general?" Jerry continued to ask.

妮妮补充道："在国家面临危难之时，将军是带领士兵奋勇杀敌的英雄，守卫着我们的家园。对于人体而言，许多疾病的发生、发展是由病邪所引起的，治疗时必须将病邪祛除体外。大黄有显著的清热、解毒、利湿、活血等祛邪作用，特别是它强大的通便功效，不但能治疗便秘，而且还能通过通便将病邪排出体外，守护人的健康。"

"大黄这么厉害呀！哇，中药治病原来有着这么多的智慧呀！"杰瑞不禁惊叹道。

Nini explained, "In times of war, a general leads soldiers in the battleground, thus guarding the country. In the human body, the key mechanism of treating diseases is to remove pathogenic factors out of the body. Rhubarb can remarkably clear heat, remove toxins, resolve dampness and circulate blood, and above all, promote bowel movements. It not only alleviates constipation, but also protects our health by removing pathogenic factors out of the body."

"How awesome rhubarb is! Wow, there is so much wisdom in Chinese medicine! " Jerry said in admiration.

大黃。

大黄 Rhubarb

产地：主产于四川、青海、甘肃等地。

性味：苦、寒。

功效：泻下通便、清热泻火、凉血解毒、活血化瘀、清利湿热。

应用：① 便秘、排便困难。

② 火热上攻出现头痛、目赤肿痛、牙龈肿痛、口臭、烦躁症状。

③ 湿热黄疸 (dǎn)、热毒皮肤疮疡、丹毒、肠痈。

④ 瘀血闭经腹痛、跌打伤痛以及血热出血，如吐血、鼻衄(nǜ)等。

Places of production: Sichuan, Qinghai, Gansu, etc.

Medicinal properties: Bitter in flavor and cold in nature.

Actions: Purges the intestine, promotes bowel movements, clears heat, reduces fire, cools blood, removes toxins, circulates blood, transforms stasis, and resolves dampness.

Indications: ① Constipation or difficulty passing stools.

② Headache, red, swollen and painful eyes, painful, swollen gums, a foul breath and restlessness due to ascending of fire heat.

③ Jaundice due to damp heat or skin sores or ulcers due to toxic heat, erysipelas and acute appendicitis.

④ Amenorrhea and abdominal pain due to stagnant blood, traumatic injuries and bleeding due to blood heat such as vomiting of blood or nosebleed.

篆书（zhuan shu）| Seal script

篆书"大"字的字形像一个张开双臂和双腿的人的形象。它的本义是顶天立地的成年人。

In the seal script, the character "大 (da)" looks like a man with open arms and legs. The original meaning is a mature, responsible man.

篆书"黄"字从字形上看像一串佩玉的样子。本义表示金子或向日葵花的颜色；引申义表示事情失败或计划不能实现等。

In the seal script, the character "黄 (huang)" looks like a string of jade beads. The original meaning is gold or a yellow color like sunflower. The extended meaning is failure to do something or failure to achieve a goal.

跟着妮妮写一写
Practice calligraphy with Nini
楷书 (kai shu) | Regular script

一 ナ 大

丶 亠 艹 艹 芺 芺 苦 昔

苗 苗 黄 黄

71

大黄茶

　　因为大黄通便特别有效，非常适
合日常服用，让我们一起来动手做一
做大黄茶吧。

　　每次称取 4-6 克大黄，加入开水
后加盖闷 5 分钟左右，服下即可，约
半小时便会起效。但需要指出的是，
以大黄通便后其色素会从小便或汗腺
中排泄，故尿液、汗液会呈现黄色，
其为服药的正常现象。

Rhubarb can significantly promote bowel movements. Let's make some rhubarb tea.

Making method: place 4-6g rhubarb in boiling water, cover the pot and wait for 5 minutes to drink. It will start working in half an hour.

Note: The pigment of rhubarb can turn urine or sweat yellow. This color change is fairly standard and typically doesn't last for long.

Rhubarb tea

妮妮和杰瑞依依不舍地告别了成都，来到了向往已久的西藏。它们一面被西藏优美的风景所吸引，一面则出现了胸闷气短、头晕乏力的高原反应。这时，当地的藏医给它们送来一瓶红景天胶囊。它们按照说明服用胶囊以后的第二天，感到神清气爽，精神饱满，继续它们在西藏的旅程。

杰瑞对此十分惊讶："妮妮，为什么这个红景天胶囊有如此神奇的作用？"

妮妮回答道："主要是红景天的作用。红景天生长在海拔 1800—2500 米的高寒无污染

Nini and Jerry reluctantly left Chengdu and came to long-awaited Tibet. While they were deeply attracted by the spectacular natural views, they experienced altitude sickness, suffering from chest tightness, shortness of breath, dizziness and fatigue. A local Tibetan doctor gave them a bottle of rhodiola capsule to alleviate the symptoms. The following day, they felt refreshed and energetic and could continue their trip in Tibet.

Jerry asked in surprise, "Nini, why is the rhodiola capsule so magical?"

Nini replied, "Because of its ingredient—rhodiola. It is a rare, wild plant that grows in a cold, unpolluted zone at an altitude of 1,800 to

地带，是珍稀野生植物。其在缺氧、低温、狂风等恶劣的环境下生长，具有强大的生命力，能够增强体质，提高身体对缺氧刺激的适应力。"

"哦。那红景天是藏药吗？应用历史悠久吗？"杰瑞继续追问。

"当然是藏药，从唐朝开始就已有应用，"妮妮继续说道，"这里还有一个在史书上有记载的关于红景天的故事。大概在距今300多年前，西藏出现了暴乱。当时的康熙皇帝御驾亲征，前往平叛。可是许多将士一到西藏

2,500 meters. The harsh environment of its growth— the rarified air low in oxygen, low temperature, and fierce wind—enables this plant to have a strong vitality. It helps to increase our physical strength and boost the body's adaptability to oxygen deficiency."

"Oh. Is rhodiola a Tibetan medicine? How long has it been used? " Jerry continued.

"Of course it is. Actually its use can be traced back to the Tang Dynasty (618-907)." Nini replied, "There is also a historical story about rhodiola. About 300 years ago, there were riots in Tibet, and Emperor Kangxi (reigned 1661–1722) personally led his soldiers in

就出现了高原反应，胸闷气短，迈不开双腿，根本无力战斗，康熙一筹莫展。恰在此时，一位藏人向康熙敬献了含有仙草的药酒。那些缺氧的将士们在服用药酒后缺氧症状迅速改善，战斗力马上恢复，很快就平息了叛乱。用于酿酒的仙草就是红景天。红景天不但可以改善缺氧状态，而且还能增强机体的抵抗力。"

"红景天真是太神奇了！"杰瑞发出了由衷的感慨。

military operations to overcome the rebellion. However, many soldiers experienced altitude sickness as soon as they arrived in Tibet. With chest tightness, shortness of breath and leg weakness, these soldiers could not fight at all. There was nothing Emperor Kangxi could do. Just at this time, a local Tibetan presented Emperor Kangxi with bottles of medicinal liquor. After drinking these medicinal liquors, the soldiers quickly recovered and defeated the rebels. It turned out that rhodiola is the medicinal herb soaked in the liquor. Rhodiola helps to increase oxygen and boost the body's natural defense."

"What an amazing plant!" Jerry said from the bottom of its heart.

红景天。

红景天 Rhodiola

产地：主要分布在东北、甘肃、四川、西藏、青海及云贵等地。

性味：甘、苦，平。

功效：益气活血，通脉平喘。

应用：① 气虚血瘀出现头痛、胸痛、胸闷以及偏瘫等症状。

② 肺脾气虚出现胸闷气喘、乏力倦怠等症状。

③ 高原反应出现头晕、胸闷、心悸、失眠、乏力等症状。

Places of production: Northeast, Gansu, Sichuan, Tibet, Qinghai, Yunnan, Guizhou, etc.

Medicinal properties: Sweet and bitter in flavor and neutral in nature.

Actions: Supplements qi, circulates blood, unblocks vessels and relieves panting.

Indications: ① Headache, chest pain/tightness and hemiplegia due to qi deficiency and blood stasis.

② Chest tightness, panting and fatigue due to qi deficiency of the lung and spleen.

③ Dizziness, chest tightness, palpitations, insomnia and fatigue due to altitude sickness.

篆书 (zhuan shu) | Seal script

"糸"通"糸、丝"。"工"既是声旁也是形旁，表示精致。"红"字本义指染成浅赤色的高级丝帛。

The 糸 is also written as "糸" or "丝 (si)". The part "工 (gong)" is both the phonetic and semantic element, meaning exquisite delicacy. The original meaning of "红 (hong)" is high-quality pale red silk.

"景"为形声字，"日"是形符，"京"是声符。本义指日光。

The character "景 (jǐng)" is pictophonetic: the top part "日 (ri)" is the semantic element and the bottom part "京 (jing)" is the phonetic element. The original meaning of this character is sunlight.

篆书"天"字从外形看像一个正面而立的人，突出了头的部分，该部分后来才简化成为一横。"天"本义指人头顶上的天空。

In the seal script, the character "天 (tian)" looks like the front view of a standing man, with the head emphasized. The original meaning of this character is sky overhead.

ㄥ ㄥ ㄠ ㄠ ㄠ ㄠ 糸 糸 紅 紅
紅

丨 冂 日 日 旦 旦 早 昙
昙 景 景 景

一 二 チ 天

81

红景天
制剂

　　到川西、青藏地区旅游已经成为当今旅游的热点之一，但其所处的高海拔却使一些人望而却步。因为川西、青藏地区地处高海拔，寒冷而氧气稀薄，许多人会由于缺氧而出现高原反应的症状。因此，在前往高原地区旅游之前，可以提前一周服用一些红景天制剂，以减缓旅行途中可能出现的高原反应症状。

The Plateau in the west of Sichuan or the eastern Tibetan Plateau is a popular destination for tourists. However, many people are concerned about its high altitude—the low temperature, rarified air low in oxygen, and possible altitude sickness. Rhodiola can tonify lung qi and increase oxygen. Therefore, it is important to take rhodiola preparations before traveling to Tibetan Plateau.

Rhodiola preparations

结束了西藏之旅，妮妮和杰瑞一路风尘仆仆，来到了齐鲁大地山东。它们拜谒了"三孔"后前往盛产金银花的平邑。妮妮和杰瑞一路走走停停，最后终于顺利抵达平邑。连日的旅行让杰瑞觉得口干舌燥，于是妮妮给它买了当地特产金银花露，杰瑞喝了后感觉好多了。

After their trip to Tibet, Nini and Jerry traveled all the way to Shandong. They first visited the temple, cemetery and family mansion of Confucius. They then arrived in Pingyi, a county of honeysuckle flowers. Jerry felt thirsty after days of traveling, so Nini bought it the local made honeysuckle flower dew. Jerry felt much better after drinking it.

突然，杰瑞指着不远处黄白相间的花问道："那是不是金银花？"

"对，那就是金银花。"妮妮答道。

杰瑞好奇地问："它为什么叫金银花？是不是因为它既有黄花又有白花？"

Suddenly, Jerry pointed at some yellowish white flowers and asked, "Are those honeysuckle flowers?"

"Yes, they are." Nini replied.

Jerry asked curiously, "Why is it called honeysuckle? Is it because it is yellowish white in color? "

妮妮笑了笑："不完全是这样的。金银花很有特色，也很迷人。它刚刚开花时是白色的，色白如银；两三天之后花色就转为黄色了，色黄如金，故名金银花，又叫二花、二宝花。此外，金银花的植株一年四季常绿，即使到了严寒的冬季也不凋谢，所以又叫'忍冬花'，而且金银花对一些临床表现上具有高热、咽痛、口干等症状都有良好的疗效呢。"

"哇，没想到金银花不仅很美，还有很多治病功效，看来金银花真是一种宝花！"杰瑞感叹道。

Nini smiled, "Not exactly. Honeysuckle is noted for its special and charming flowers. The flowers start with sliver white and turn golden yellow after a couple of days. That is how it gets the Chinese name Jinyinhua, which literally means gold and silver flower. It is also known as the double flower or the double treasure flower. In addition, it has another name Rendonghua (literally means cold-tolerant flower) since this evergreen plant thrives in all seasons, including cold winter. Clinically, honeysuckle flowers work well for high-grade fever, sore throat and a dry mouth.

"Wow, honeysuckle flowers are both beautiful and therapeutic, and indeed a treasure flower!" Jerry exclaimed.

金银花。

金银花 ○Honeysuckle

产地：主产于山东、河南、江西、浙江、湖
　　　南等地。
性味：甘寒。
功效：清热解毒，疏散风热。
应用：① 风热感冒、流感出现发热、咽痛、
　　　头痛等症状。
　　　② 皮肤疮病痛肿，局部皮肤红肿热痛。

Places of production: Shandong, Henan, Jiangxi, Zhejiang, Hunan, etc.

Medicinal properties: Sweet in flavor and cold in nature.

Actions: Clears heat, removes toxins, dispels wind.

Indications: ① Fever, sore throat and headache in common cold (due to
wind heat) or influenza.

② Red, warm, swollen and painful skin sores, ulcers or boils.

篆书 (zhuan shu) | Seal script

会意字，从"仐"，表示覆盖、冶炼；从"土"，表示藏在地下。本义指金属。

An associative compound: the "亼" means to cover or smelt metal, the "土 (tu)" means hidden underground. The original meaning of this character is metal.

篆书"银"字为形声字，"金"是形符，"艮"是声符。银指白银，引申指作为通货的银币或银子，又指像银子一样的颜色。

In the seal script, "银 (yin)" is a pictophonetic character. The "金 (jin)" is the semantic element, meaning silver or silver color. It is later used to refer to silver coins for currency. The "艮" is the phonetic element.

"花"字从外形看像一棵树上繁花盛开的样子。本义是树上开的花，引申为"美丽"。

The character "花 (hua)" looks like flowers blossoming in a tree. The original meaning is tree flowers. The extended meaning is beauty.

丿 人 人 仐 仐 余
金 金

丿 丿 上 午 午 钅 金
钊 钊 钊 钽 银 银

一 十 廾 艹 艼 花 花

金银花
栽培

　　金银花的适应能力很强，喜欢强光照射，并且也能够耐寒，冬季在室外越冬也不是问题。虽然金银花常生长在山坡上，但是近年来越来越多的人开始在家里盆栽金银花了。

　　将准备好的金银花小苗栽种到盆土中，并浇好水，然后放置在阴凉通风处。

Honeysuckle has a strong adaptability. It thrives in sites exposed to direct sunlight. It is cold-tolerant so it can survive outdoors in winter. Although honeysuckle often grows on slopes or hillsides, many people start to plant it indoors.

Plant honeysuckle seeds into a pot, keep them watered and place it in a shady area with good ventilation.

Honeysuckle cultivation

离开山东，妮妮和杰瑞决定去探访中国四大古城之一的山西平遥古城。在前往山西的高铁上杰瑞生病了，发热、头痛、咽痛、鼻塞流涕。妮妮认为杰瑞患了流感，便给它服用随身携带的双黄连口服液。杰瑞服用了两支双黄连口服液后，在宾馆昏昏沉沉睡了一觉，一觉醒来，感觉好了很多，烧也退了。

它很惊讶地问："这个双黄连口服液中有什么成分，是不是黄连？"

妮妮笑道："不是。双黄连其实是由三味中药的第一个字组成：双是双花，就是前面

After leaving Shandong, Nini and Jerry decided to visit Pingyao in Shanxi Province, one of the four ancient cities in China. Jerry got sick on the high-speed train to Shanxi. It presented with fever, headache, sore throat, runny nose and nasal congestion. Nini believed that Jerry caught a bad flu and gave it the Shuanghuanglian Oral Liquid. After taking two vials of the Oral Liquid, Jerry fell asleep in the hotel. When it woke up, it felt a lot better and its fever was gone.

It asked in surprise, "What are the ingredients in this Shuanghuanglian Oral Liquid? Is it coptis?"

Nini laughed, "No. Shuanghuanglian got the name from initials of the three kinds of ingredients: Shuanghua (also known as Jinyinhua,

提到的金银花；黄是黄芩；连是连翘。"

"这药名取得真好。那双黄连口服液的作用是不是就是这三种药物作用的综合？"杰瑞有点刨根问底。

"可以这么说，但也有不同之处。双黄连口服液的主要作用就是清热解毒、疏散风热，而这是金银花与连翘的共同作用，可以用于流感的预防和治疗。"妮妮回答。

"那金银花与连翘的功用有什么区别吗？"杰瑞继续问道。

"有的。金银花与连翘的清热解毒、疏散

honeysuckle flower), Huangqin (Scutellaria root) and Lianqiao (fructus forsythiae)."

"That's a good name. So the actions of the Shuanghuanglian Oral Liquid are just the adding up of actions of the three ingredients? " Asked Jerry, trying to get to the bottom of it.

"In a way, you could say that, but not entirely. The main actions of Shuanghuanglian Oral Liquid are to clear heat, remove toxins and dispel wind through the joint functions of honeysuckle and fructus forsythiae. It can be used for influenza prevention and treatment."

"Are there any different actions between honeysuckle and fructus forsythiae?" Jerry continued.

"Yes. They both can clear heat, remove toxins and dispel wind. As a

风热作用类似，因此在治疗流感时常常配合使用。但相对而言，金银花的清热解毒作用更强，其所治疗热毒引起的疾病更为广泛。连翘的清热解毒作用有一个特点，其还能消痈散结，善于治疗疔疮。此外，连翘还有一定的利尿作用，能够把热毒等病邪从小便中排出。因此，在治疗一些呼吸道的传染性疾病时，金银花与连翘同用，作用就大大增强，起到一加一大于二的效果。"妮妮向杰瑞分析说。

"原来如此。"杰瑞恍然大悟。说罢便与妮妮一起，兴高采烈地继续踏上了平遥古城之旅。

result, the two are often used in combination for influenza. Comparatively, honeysuckle has a stronger and more extensive effect on removing toxins, while fructus forsythiae helps resolve boils, sores, or ulcers. In addition, fructus forsythiae can induce urination and thus remove toxic heat through urine. That is why the two herbs are often used in combination to achieve a synergistic effect (one plus one equals more than two) for infectious respiratory diseases including Covid-19." Nini explained to Jerry.

"So that's it." Jerry said to Nini. Then they continued their trip to the ancient city Pingyao.

连翘。

连翘 ○ Fructus forsythiae

产地：主产于山西、河南、山东等地。

性味：苦，微寒。

功效：清热解毒，消痈散结，疏散风热。

应用：① 流感、禽流感等出现发热、头身痛、
咽痛等症状。

② 皮肤疮疡痈肿，局部皮肤红肿热痛、
疔疮。

③ 瘰疬 (luǒ lì) 结核。

基本信息 ─●
Essential information

Places of production: Shanxi, Henan, Shandong, etc.

Medicinal properties: Bitter in flavor and mildly warm in nature.

Actions: Clears heat, removes toxins, resolves boils/nodules, and dispels wind.

Indications: ① Fever, body ache, headache and sore throat in influenza
and bird flu, etc.

② Red, warm, swollen and painful skin sores, ulcers or boils.

③ Tuberculosis of cervical lymph nodes.

篆书 (zhuan shu) | Seal script

篆书"连"字为会意字。从"辵"，从"车"。本义指人拉车行走。

In the seal script, "连 (lian)" is an associative character. It consisits of "辵 (chuo)" and "车 (che)". The original meaning is walking and pulling a jinrikisha.

形声字，"羽"是形符，"尧"是声符。有举起、抬起、向上的释义。

A pictophonetic character: "羽(yu)" is the semantic element and "尧(yao)" is the phonetic element. It means to raise or lift up.

跟着妮妮写一写
Practice calligraphy with Jerry
楷书 (kai shu) | Regular script

一 厂 厅 百 百 車 車 連 連 連

一 十 土 井 井 井 走 走 走 走 尧 尧 尧 尭 翹 翹 翹

双黄连
口服液

双黄连口服液对于一些呼吸道传染性疾病的防治有着很好的作用,在日常生活中也成为许多家庭的常备药物之一。不过,如果问及"双黄连口服液"的主要成分是什么,很多人会毫不犹豫地回答是"黄物组成的,"双"是指双花,也就是黄金银花,而"黄连"并非是一味黄连,而是指黄芩和连翘。

The Shuanghuanglian Oral Liquid works well for infectious respiratory diseases. It's now become a common household medicine. Many people may think Huanglian (rhizoma coptidis) is the major ingredient of the Oral Liquid. This is not the case. Actually it got the name from initials of the three ingredients: Shuanghua (also known as Jinyinhua, honeysuckle flower), Huangqin (scutellaria root) and Lianqiao (fructus forsythia).

Shuanghuanglian
Oral Liquid

时间过得很快，转眼已到了深秋，北方已经开始下雪，妮妮和杰瑞想再去领略一下北方的寒冷。于是，它们一路北上，来到了内蒙古。

一天，它们发现一个十分奇特的现象：虽然大地上被冰雪覆盖，可是在一种发黄的植物四周则地面干燥，几无积雪结冰。

杰瑞很是惊讶，不解地问道："妮妮，这个是什么植物啊？为什么在它周围都没有冰雪呢？"

Time flies. It was now late autumn and snow had begun to fall in the north. Nini and Jerry wanted to experience the chilly winter there, so they traveled all the way to Inner Mongolia.

One day, they noticed an odd thing — although the earth was covered in ice and snow, there was dry ground around a yellow plant.

Jerry was surprised and puzzled, "Nini, what kind of plant is this? How come there is no snow around it?"

"杰瑞，你知道吗？这个植物是一味著名的中药，叫麻黄。有强大的发汗力，并通过发汗而散寒，这与它本身的性质有关。麻黄体内是温热的，而且还能将温热之气向四周发散，所以麻黄的四周不会积雪结冰。"妮妮解释道。

"是不是说麻黄能将自身体内的热量向四周发散，才使它四周的温度增高，从而驱散寒气，不积冰雪，它作用于人体时就能发散寒气？"杰瑞若有所悟地说道。突然，它好像又想起了什么："可是如果麻黄一直向外发散自己的热能，会不会到最后因此而死亡呢？"

"Jerry, this plant is a famous Chinese herb called ephedra. It can strongly induce sweating to dissipate cold, because it is warm in nature. Since it also disperses warmth and heat outward, so that is why there is no snow or ice around it." Nini explained.

"Does that mean ephedra can dissipate cold in human body because it can dissipate cold in natural world by dispersing warmth outward?" Jerry said insightfully. But suddenly it seemed to think of something else, "If ephedra has kept dispersing its own heat or warmth, will it eventually die from it?"

妮妮笑了笑："不会的，因为麻黄的结构很有意思。具有发汗作用的是麻黄的茎，而麻黄的节与根则具有止汗作用。这样一来，麻黄茎发汗，麻黄根和节止汗，以便确保麻黄草的平衡而正常生长。"

"大自然真是太奇妙了！"杰瑞感叹道，"妮妮，如果有人出现发热的症状了，是不是就可以服用这味药？"

"对呀，杰瑞。同时，麻黄还被古人誉为'喘家圣药'，有十分显著的止咳平喘的作用。"杰瑞一边观察着麻黄，一边听妮妮给它讲关于麻黄的这些事。

Nini smiled and said, "No, it won't. Ephedra has an interestingly balanced structure. Its stem induces sweating; however, its nodes and roots stop sweating. In this way, this herb can grow normally."

"Nature is so amazing and wonderful!" Jerry exclaimed, "Nini, so people with a fever can take this herb?"

"Yes, Jerry. This herb is also known as a 'holy medicine for asthma' in ancient times because of its remarkable effects on alleviating cough and panting." Jerry studied this magical plant while listening to Nini.

麻黄。

麻黄 Ephedra

产地：主产于内蒙古、甘肃、山西、河北等地。

性味：辛，温。

功效：发汗散寒，宣肺平喘，利尿消肿。

应用：① 风寒感冒出现恶寒、头身痛。
② 咳喘，尤其是受寒后的咳喘。
③ 急性水肿。

Places of production: Inner Mongolia, Gansu, Shanxi, Hebei, etc.

Medicinal properties: Pungent in flavor and warm in nature.

Actions: Induces sweating, dissipates cold, disperses lung qi, alleviates panting, promotes urination and resolves swelling.

Indications: ① Chills, body ache and headache in common cold (due to wind cold).

② Cough and panting after exposure to cold.

③ Acute edema.

跟着妮妮学一学
Learn calligraphy with Nini

篆书（zhuan shu）| Seal script

　　篆书"麻"字的上部表示敞屋，下部是一缕缕纤麻的形状。本义指一种野生植物。

In the seal script, the top part of "麻 (ma)" means spacious house, and the bottom, woody fibers. This character means wild plants growing on cliffs.

　　篆书"黄"字从字形上看像一串佩玉的样子。本义表示金子或向日葵花的颜色；引申义表示事情失败或计划不能实现等。

In the seal script, the character "黄 (huang)" looks like a string of jade beads. The original meaning is gold or a yellow color like sunflowers. The extended meaning is failure to do something or failure to achieve a goal.

跟着妮妮写一写
Practice calligraphy with Nini
楷书（kai shu）| Regular script

`丶 亠 广 广 庐 庐 床 床 府 府 麻`

`丶 十 艹 艹 艹 芷 苎 苦 莳 莳 黄 黄`

麻黄的应用有一个常需要引起关注的现象，那就是麻黄不同的药用部位具有相反的功效。具有发汗作用的是麻黄茎，而麻黄根和麻黄节不但没有发汗作用，反而是止汗、治疗多汗的专药。日常应用麻黄十分简单，可直接泡水冲饮。

麻黄饮品

It is worth noting that different parts of ephedra have opposite functions: its stem induces sweating, while its nodes and roots stop sweating. In everyday life, we can place ephedra in hot water and drink it like tea.

Ephedra drink ─●

妮妮与杰瑞中国之旅的最后一站是东北。高铁上，妮妮神秘地问杰瑞："杰瑞，你听说过东北三宝吗？"

　　"当然知道，人参、貂皮、鹿茸，"杰瑞骄傲地回答，"我还知道三宝中的人参和鹿茸是著名的中药。"

　　"你知道得真多。那你还知道其他主产于东北的中药吗？特别是有一味中药对于流感、禽流感有很好的预防和治疗作用，你知道是什么吗？"妮妮继续问。

The last stop of their China trip is northeastern China. On the high-speed train, Nini mysteriously asked Jerry, "Jerry, have you heard of the three treasures of northeastern China?"

"Of course, ginseng, sable fur, and pilose antler," Jerry replied proudly, "I also know that ginseng and pilose antler are two famous Chinese medicines."

"Good for you, Jerry. Do you know any other Chinese medicines mainly produced in northeastern China? One herb is particularly effective in influenza and bird flu prevention and treatment. Do you know what it is?" Nini continued to ask.

杰瑞想了想，摇摇头："我不知道。你快告诉我，那是什么药？"

"贯众。"妮妮说。

"贯众是不是也像金银花、连翘、板蓝根一样有清热解毒的功效？"杰瑞似懂非懂地问。

"对，但不完全是。贯众解毒的特点在于善于清解来自于自然界的时行疫气。"妮妮说。

"什么是时行疫气？"杰瑞不解地问。

Jerry shook its head, "No, I don't. You tell me."

"Rhizoma cyrtomii." said Nini.

"Can this herb clear heat and remove toxins just like honeysuckle, forsythia and isatis root?" Jerry did not fully understand.

"Yes, but not exactly the same. Rhizoma cyrtomii is more effective in clearing seasonal epidemic qi. " Nini said.

"What is epidemic qi?" Jerry was puzzled.

"每年春夏季节，自然界中常会产生一些毒性物质，通过侵犯人体而引发一些类似于流感的传染性疾病，这就是所谓的时行疫气。贯众自古以来就被认为是防治时行疫气的药。曾有记载，古时候将贯众浸泡在水缸里，水缸里的饮用水就能预防瘟疫。因为贯众苦寒并有小毒，既能清热解毒又能以毒攻毒，并能凉血杀虫，故而对时行疫气有十分显著的防治作用。"妮妮耐心地解释。

"现在我终于明白了。虽然都能清热解毒，但每味药物的作用特点不一样。"杰瑞恍然大悟。

"Seasonal epidemic qi often occurs in spring and summer. It may affect the human body and cause contagious diseases such as influenza. Rhizoma cyrtomii has long been used to prevent and treat epidemic qi. It has been recorded that in ancient times, people soaked this plant in water and then drank the water to prevent pestilence. Rhizoma cyrtomii is bitter in flavor, cold in nature, and mildly toxic. It clears heat, removes toxins and fights toxins with toxins. In addition, it cools blood and kills parasites. Therefore, it has remarkable effects on epidemic qi prevention and treatment. " Nini explained patiently.

"Now I see. All these herbs can clear heat and remove toxins, but each is different and special in its own way." Jerry finally understands.

贯众。

贯众 ○ Rhizoma cyrtomii

产地：主产于黑龙江、吉林、辽宁。

性味：苦，微寒；有小毒。

功效：清热解毒，杀虫。

应用：① 风热感冒、时行感冒出现发热、咽痛、头痛等症状，如流感、禽流感。
② 热毒斑疹，痄(zhà)腮(流行性腮腺炎)。
③ 肠道寄生虫病。

Places of production: Heilongjiang, Jilin, Liaoning, etc.

Medicinal properties: Bitter in flavor, mildly cold in nature and mildly toxic.

Actions: Clears heat, removes toxins and kills parasites.

Indications: ① Fever, sore throat, headache in common cold or influenza and bird flu.
② Maculae due to toxic heat or mumps (epidemic parotitis).
③ Intestinal parasitic infections.

篆书 (zhuan shu) | Seal script

篆书"贯"为会意字。本义是指以绳串贝、以绳串线。引申为"贯穿"。

The "贯 (guan)" is an associative character. The original meaning is to string seashells using a rope or to string coins using a rope. The extended meaning is convergent.

甲骨文"众"字的上部表示日(太阳),字的下部表示三个并立的人。在古代中国,"三"不仅表示数字"三",更可以表示"多数"或"多次"的意思。本义表示在太阳之下有很多人。

In the oracle-bone inscriptions, the top part of "众 (zhong)" signals the sun, and the bottom part means three people standing together. In ancient China, besides the number of three, the word "three" often means many. The original meaning of this character is that many people standing under the sun.

跟着妮妮写一写
Practice calligraphy with Nini
楷书 (kai shu) | Regular script

乚 乛 夕 母 母 毌 冑 冑 冑
冑 賈 賈

丿 亻 冂 的 血 血 尔 尔 尔
尔 尔 衆

贯众
种植

如今很多家庭不仅种植一些鲜花，也开始培植一些类似于树木类的植物。比如贯众，它不仅可以在户外种植，也是非常好的室内观赏植物。

我们只要在日常养护的过程中保证最低温度不要低于五度，并每隔三五天喷水来保证空气湿度即可，由于北方空气相对干燥，可以每天喷水。

Today, in addition to flowers, fern plants like rhizoma cyrtomii are starting to become popular. They can grow outdoors in the garden or indoors as houseplants, since their green leaves can add beauty to the room.

They are easy to grow and care for. All they need is to keep the room temperature at above 5°C and keep them watered every 3-5 days to ensure that there is plenty of humidity. People in northern China may need to spray water to them daily to help them grow well.

Rhizoma Cyrtomii cultivation

游历完大半个中国，妮妮和杰瑞乘飞机回到了上海。傍晚回到宾馆，杰瑞感到非常疲劳，有点发烧，咽痛发干。它很担心第二天不能乘飞机回国，妮妮也有点着急，赶紧到附近的一家中药店买药。

　　很快，妮妮买了一盒润喉糖和一包绿色的叶子回来。它对杰瑞说："你先吃这个润喉糖，我去烧点水冲泡这个叶子。"

　　"嗯。"杰瑞听话地将一颗润喉糖含在嘴里，立马感到口里有一股清凉感，透过咽喉、鼻腔直冲脑门，疼痛、紧绷的喉咙也很快清爽

After traveling more than half of China, Nini and Jerry flew back to Shanghai. When they got back to the hotel in the evening, Jerry felt very tired. It also had a mild fever and a dry, sore throat. It became worried about the long flight the next day. Nini anxiously went to a nearby pharmacy to buy medicine.

Soon, Nini came back with a box of throat lozenges and a packet of green leaves. It said to Jerry, "Take the throat lozenge first, and I will boil some water to brew these leaves."

"Okay." Jerry put a throat lozenge in its mouth. Almost immediately a cooling sensation started in the mouth and then rushed up to the nose

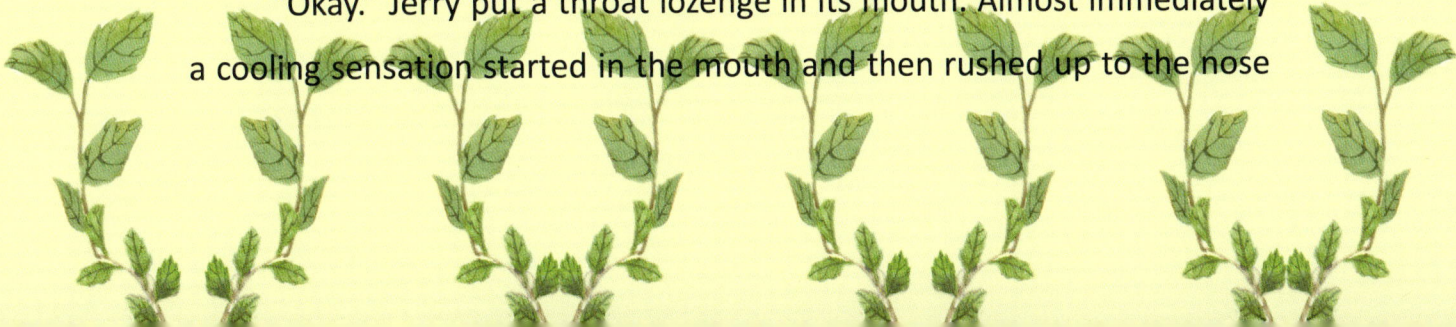

了一些。"天啊，这个润喉糖怎么这么神奇！"杰瑞兴奋地喊了起来。

不一会儿，杰瑞闻到一股弥漫在房间里的清香味。妮妮端着一碗热气腾腾的汤水来到杰瑞床前说："你趁热将这碗汤水喝下去，然后捂着被子睡一觉，微微出一身汗就好了。"

杰瑞端起碗，闻了闻，只觉得一阵清香扑鼻而来。它似乎有点不舍地慢慢喝下了汤水，捂紧被子躺了下去，很快进入了梦乡。

一觉醒来，杰瑞神清气爽，咽痛、发烧消失了，十分高兴地对妮妮说："我可以回国了！"然后他又有些好奇地问妮妮，"昨晚你

and forehead. Its sore, tight throat was somewhat relieved. "Oh dear, this throat lozenge is amazing!" Jerry shouted excitedly.

After a while, Jerry smelled a pleasant scent that permeated the room. Nini took a bowl of hot, steaming soup to Jerry's bed and said, "Drink the hot soup, cover up with a blanket to sleep, and you will be fine after a little bit sweating."

Jerry picked up the bowl and sniffed it, breathing in the sweet fragrance. It drank the soup slowly, covered up with blanket and went to sleep.

When it woke up, Jerry felt refreshed, and its sore throat and fever disappeared. It said to Nini happily, "I am glad that I can go back home."

给我吃的是什么润喉糖和汤水呀？为啥如此有效？"

"是薄荷的作用，润喉糖和汤水的主要成分都是薄荷。与上海邻近的江苏产的薄荷质量最好，称为苏薄荷。薄荷性质清凉，质地轻清，善于宣发，清利五官，有一定的发汗作用，非常适合用于风热感冒、轻度流感的治疗。"妮妮说。

"薄荷这么有用啊，我回家也要种。"杰瑞暗暗下决心。

Then it asked Nini curiously, "What lozenges and soup did you give me last night? Why are they so effective? "

Nini said, "The key is mint, the major ingredient of the throat lozenges and soup. Neighbouring Shanghai, Jiangsu Province has the best quality mint across China. Mint has a cool property and acts to disperse qi and help induce sweating. It is often used for common cold (due to wind heat) and mild influenza."

"Mint is so great and beneficial. I'm going to plant it when I go home." Jerry made up its mind silently.

薄荷。

薄荷 ○ Mint

产地：全国多地产，江苏所产最佳。

性味：辛，凉。

功效：发散风热，清利咽喉.透疹止痒，疏畅肝气。

应用：① 风热感冒，流感出现发热、头痛、咽痛。

② 头面部风热病证出现头痛、牙痛、目赤肿痛、咽痛不适。

③ 麻疹、风疹初期疹出不畅、皮肤瘙痒。

④ 肝郁不舒出现胁痛。

Places of production: Multiple areas in China, especially Jiangsu (the best quality).

Medicinal properties: Pungent in flavor and cool in nature.

Actions: Dispels wind, clears heat, benefits the throat, accelerates eruption of skin rashes, stops itching, and regulates liver qi.

Indications: ① Fever, headache and sore throat in common cold (due to wind heat) or influenza.

② Headache, toothache, red, swollen and painful eyes, and sore throat due to wind heat affecting the head and face.

③ Inhibited eruption of skin rashes and itchy skin in the early stage of measles/rubella.

④ Pain in the costal region due to liver qi stagnation.

篆书 (zhuan shu) ｜ Seal script

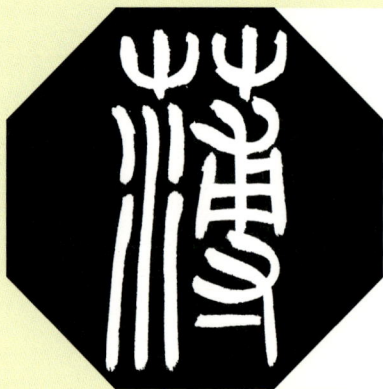

　　篆书"薄"为形声字，"草"字的上部表示这是草本植物，是形符。下部分"薄"为声符。本义是草木丛生的地方。

In the seal script, "薄 (bo)" is a pictophonetic character. The top part "艹" is the semantic element, meaning grass or plant. The bottom part "溥" is the phonetic element. The original meaning of character "薄" is a place covered with grass or bushes.

　　篆书"荷"为形声字，"草"字的上部表示这是草本植物，是形符。下部分"何"字是声符。本义为植物名，也称莲，别称芙蕖、芙蓉。

In the seal script, "荷" is a pictophonetic character. The top (semantic) part "艹" is the semantic element, meaning grass. The bottom part "何 (he)" is the phonetic element. The original meaning of character "荷" is a plant, also known as "莲 (lian)", which has two other names— "芙蕖 (fu qu)" and "芙蓉 (fu rong)".

丶 亠 艹 艹 艹 艹 艹 艹
艹 荢 荢 蒲 蒲 蒲 蒲 薄
薄

丶 亠 艹 艹 艹 芢 荷 荷
荷 荷 荷

131

动手做一做 ○

薄荷栽培

薄荷喜温暖湿润的环境。最佳生长温度为20－30℃，其生命力旺盛，适应性强，耐寒而易种植，如今在家中用一些芳香类的草木花卉装点居室也成为现代人追求生活品质的主要方式，而薄荷是其中不错的选择。

在家栽培薄荷时注意多浇水，定期对土壤疏松通风。

Mint likes a warm and moist environment. The optimal growth temperature is 20–30°C. This fragrant herb is very easy to grow. Its prolific nature and strong adaptability makes it a great option for growing indoors.

Mint requires little care other than keeping it watered and regularly loosening the soil.

Mint
cultivation

历时半年多时间的中国之行就要结束了，杰瑞将返回自己的国家，妮妮前往机场送行，两位好朋友难舍难分。

　　没想到，杰瑞回国后半年，就发生了新冠疫情，它想到了妮妮的爷爷是著名的老中医，给妮妮写信求援，把周边的小伙伴们的不同病情告诉妮妮，妮妮请爷爷配好药，寄给杰瑞，杰瑞把这些中药送给了需要的朋友。虽然它们暂时不能见面了，但是它们的友谊并没有因此中断，它们相约等疫情结束后继续见面。

The six-month trip in China is coming to an end. It was time for Jerry to return to its home country. Nini went to the airport to see it off, and the two friends sadly said goodbye.

Unfortunately, the Covid-19 pandemic broke out half a year after Jerry returned home. Knowing that Nini's grandfather is a famous TCM doctor, Jerry asked for help by writing to Nini about its friends' health conditions. Then Nini sent medicines prepared by its grandfather to Jerry and its friends in need. Although Nini and Jerry cannot see each other for the time being, their hearts are still connected. They will definitely catch up after the pandemic is over.

后记

"书法小联合国"中华文化特色教材《风调雨顺：春夏秋冬》、《风调雨顺：十二生肖》五种中英文读物，近期已被海外出版社翻译为多个语种版本，在国际社会产生了积极影响，正如第八任联合国秘书长、博鳌亚洲论坛理事长潘基文先生为该丛书所作的推荐词所言："周斌教授编写的《风调雨顺》系列丛书，是一套让全世界人民都可以来参与书法和文化学习的好书。"

2020年是令人难忘的一年，新冠疫情在世界各国蔓延，中国在疫情控制与疾病治疗方面取得了令人瞩目的成绩，其中，中医药在治疗新冠疾病中发挥了积极作用。我在这一年有幸被聘为上海中医药大学特聘教授、"中医药文化国际传播大使"。在上海中医药大学徐建光校长与上海市中医药管理局胡鸿毅副局长等专家的鼓励下，在上海交通大学文创学院张伟民院长的大力支持下，我与著名中医药学专家杨柏灿教授共同商讨，经过近一年的努力，终于完成了《风调雨顺：国风》的撰写工作。

《风调雨顺：国风》，以趣味性故事为线索，将中医药文化植入到文化旅游的语境中，结合汉字文化和书写艺术，浅显易懂地对传统文化进行解读，通过中英文双语形式以及融媒体技术，向世界人民介绍优秀的中华文化。

"书法小联合国"是在时任联合国秘书长潘基文先生的鼎立支持下，于2014年4月在联合国总部创立的，经过多年的努力，目前已成为联合国新闻媒体部下的NGO组织。此次将中医药文化纳入到"书法小联合国"中华文化特色教材的系统之中，相信会在传播与推广中医药文化等方面起到独特的作用。

感谢第八任联合国秘书长潘基文先生为该丛书撰写的推荐词，感谢上海中医药大学徐建光校长、上海交通大学黄震副校长、上海市中医药管理局胡鸿毅副局长、上海中医药大学陈红专副校长与上海交通大学文创学院张伟民院长等专家的大力支持！感谢上海中医药大学校长办公室张怡副主任、教务处舒静处长以及上海中医药博物馆李赣馆长的鼎立协助，感谢华东师范大学出版社王焰社长、龚海燕副社长在该书出版过程中提供的帮助，在该丛书的撰写过程中也得到了杨熠文博士等学者的帮助。

《风调雨顺：国风》是我们结合文化旅游进行中医药科普的一次尝试，在专家委员会的支持下，我们还将陆续出版《风调雨顺》中医药文化系列丛书，为中医药文化的国际分享作出贡献。

周　斌

于上海交通大学上海交大–南加州大学文化创意产业学院

中国书法文化国际传播研究所

2021年3月

Afterword

The 5 bilingual (Chinese/English) book set supported by the *Junior United Nations of Calligraphy —Feng Tiao Yu Shun* (literally means peace and prosperity comes with pleasant wind and timely rain): spring, summer, autumn, winter and the Chinese Zodiac, have been translated into multiple languages. Mr. Ban Ki-moon, the former UN Secretary-General and the chairman of the Boao Forum for Asia once said, "The *Feng Tiao Yu Shun* book set written by Prof. Zhou Bin provided a perfect textbook for people around the world studying Chinese calligraphy and culture".

The year 2020 witnessed the remarkable achievement in the control and treatment of Covid-19 amid its spread throughout the world. Traditional Chinese medicine played an active role in the battle against the pandemic. During this year, I was honored to be appointed as a guest professor by Shanghai University of Traditional Chinese Medicine and an Ambassador for International Communication of Chinese Medicine and Culture. Also in this year, through the joint effort with Prof. Yang Bai-can, a well-known Chinese medicine expert, we completed the book *Feng Tiao Yu Shun—Guo Feng.* My sincere gratitude goes to Dr. Xu Jianguang, President of Shanghai University of Traditional Chinese Medicine (SHUTCM), Dr. Hu Hongyi, Vice director general of Shanghai Municipal Administration of Traditional Chinese Medicine, and Dr. Zhang Weimin, Dean of Shanghai Jiaotong University Institute of Cultural and Creative Industry.

This bilingual (Chinese/English) book uses interesting stories to explain Chinese medicinal herbs, along with calligraphy and interpretation of Chinese characters.

Thanks to the support of Mr. Ban Ki-moon, the then UN Secretary-General, the Junior United Nations of Calligraphy was established at the United Nations headquarters in April 2014. Today it has become a United Nations NGO program within the UN News & Media Division. I firmly believe that this book will contribute to the promotion of Chinese medicine and culture.

My sincere gratitude also goes to Mr. Ban Ki-moon, Mr. Huang Zhen, Vice President of Shanghai Jiaotong University, Prof. Chen Hongzhuan, Vice President of SHUTCM, Ms Zhang Yi, Vice Director of the President's

Office, SHUTCM, Ms Shu Jing, Head of Academic Affairs, SHUTCM, Mr. Li Gan, Director of Shanghai TCM Museum, Mr. Wang Yan, President of East China Normal University Press, Ms Gong Haiyan, Vice President of East China Normal University Press, and Dr. Yang Yiwen.

This book is an example of combining the knowledge of Chinese medicine with cultural tourism. We will continue to publish more books for readers from both home and abroad.

Zhou Bin

University of South California (USC)−Shanghai Jiaotong University (SJTU)

Institute of Cultural and Creative Industry

Chinese Calligraphy Culture Education and Communication Center

板蓝根 藿香 鱼腥草

杏仁 甘草 石膏 大黄

红景天 金银花 连翘

麻黄 贯众 薄荷

板 板 板

板 板

藍

①②③④⑤⑥⑦⑧⑨⑩⑪⑫⑬⑭⑮⑯⑰⑱⑲

根　根　根

根　根

藿

① ② ③ ④ ⑤ ⑥ ⑦ ⑧ ⑨ ⑩ ⑪ ⑫ ⑬ ⑭ ⑮ ⑯ ⑰ ⑱ ⑲

藿

藿

藿

香　香　香①
　　　　②③④⑤⑥⑦⑧⑨

香　香

魚　魚　魚

①②③④⑤⑥⑦⑧⑨⑩⑪

魚　魚

腥　腥　腥

腥　腥

草　草　草

①②③④⑤⑥⑦⑧⑨⑩

草　草

杏　杏　杏

杏　杏

仁 仁 仁

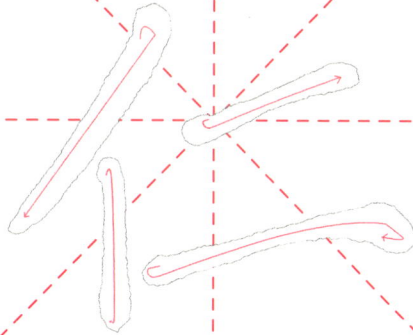

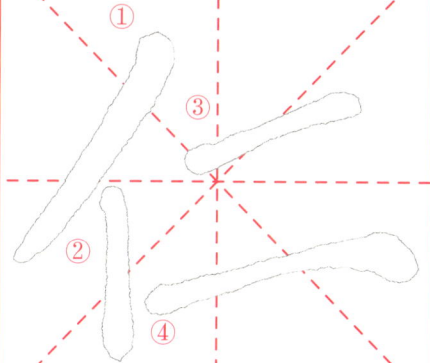

① ③ ② ④

仁 仁

甘　甘　甘
甘　甘

草　草　草

草　草

① ② ③ ④ ⑤ ⑥ ⑦ ⑧ ⑨ ⑩

石 石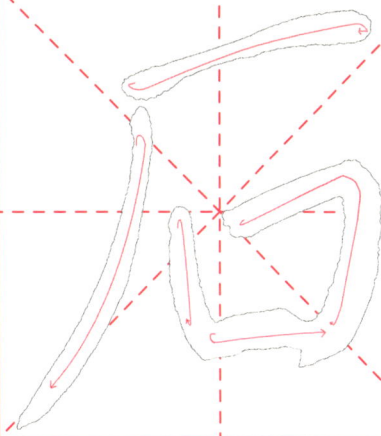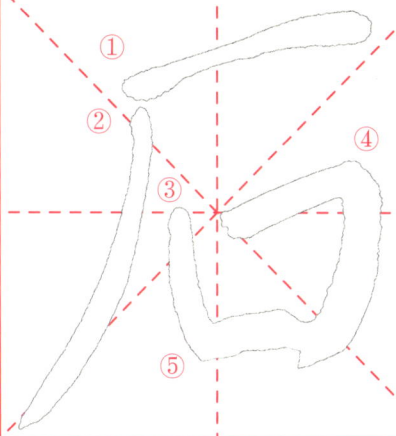

石 石

膏 膏 膏
膏 膏

大　大　大

①　②　③

大　大

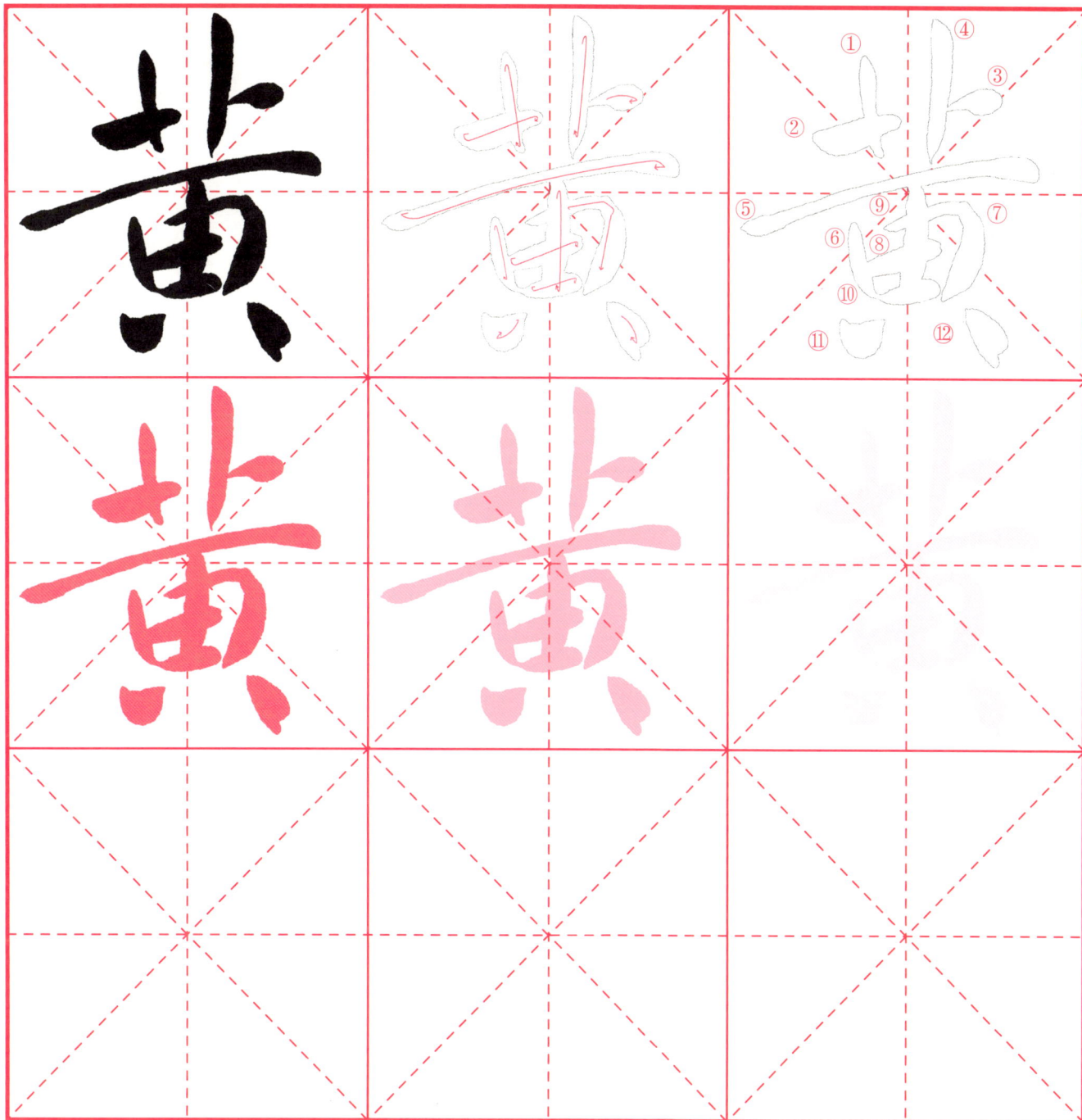

黄　黄　黄

黄　黄

红　红　红
红　红　红

景　景　景

景　景

①②③④⑤⑥⑦⑧⑨⑩⑪⑫

天 天 天
天 天

①②③④

金　金　金

金　金

銀　銀　銀

①　②
⑨
⑫　⑩
③　⑪
⑤　⑬
④　⑦
⑥
⑧
⑭

銀　銀

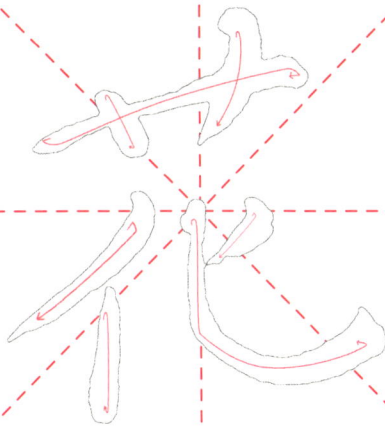
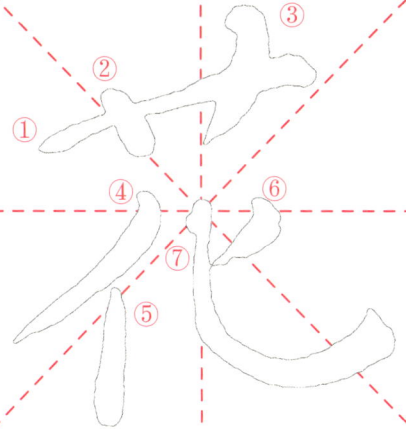
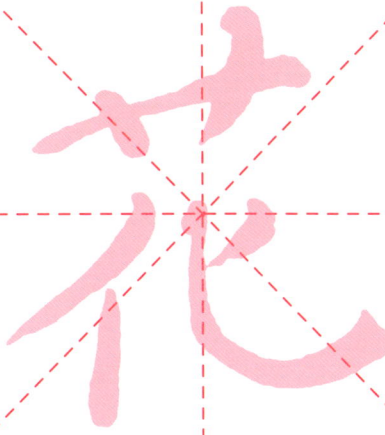
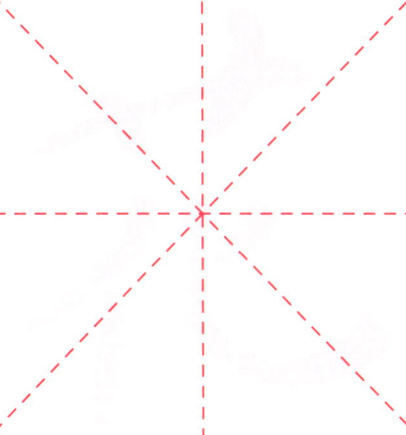

連　連　連
連　連

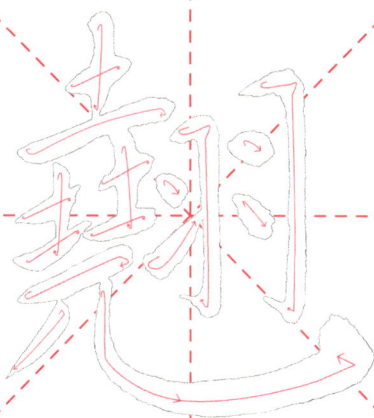

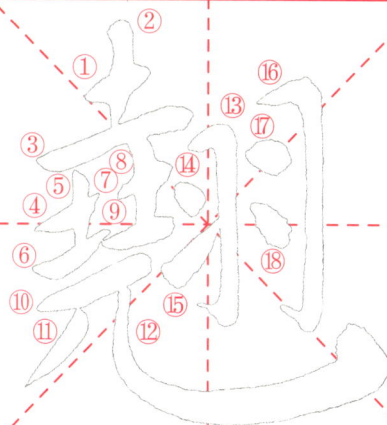

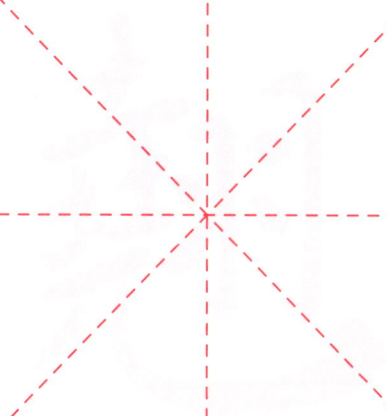

麻 麻 麻
麻 麻 麻

①②③④⑤⑥⑦⑧⑨⑩⑪

黄　黄

黄　黄

贵

衆

薄

荷　荷　荷

荷　荷